The Family Therapy Collections

James C. Hansen, Series Editor

Florence W. Kaslow, Volume Editor

COUPLES THERAPY IN A FAMILY CONTEXT

Perspective and Retrospective

AN ASPEN PUBLICATION®
Aspen Publishers, Inc.
Rockville, Maryland
Royal Tunbridge Wells
1988

Library of Congress Cataloging-in-Publication Data

Couples therapy in a family context : perspective and retrospective /
Florence W. Kaslow, volume editor.
p. cm. — (The Family therapy collections ; 25)
"An Aspen publication."
Includes bibliographies and index.
ISBN: 0-87189-756-3
1. Marital psychotherapy. I. Kaslow, Florence Whiteman.
II. Series.
RC488.5.C69   1988
616.89′156--dc19

87-35116
CIP

The Family Therapy Collections series is indexed in *Psychological Abstracts* and the PsycINFO database

Article reprints are available from University Microfilms International,
300 North Zeeb Road, Dept., A.R.S., Ann Arbor, MI 48106.

Editorial Services: Ruth Bloom

Library of Congress Catalog Card Number: 87-35116 CIP
ISBN: 0-87189-7563
ISSN: 0735-9152

Printed in the United States of America

1 2 3 4 5

Table of Contents

Board of Editors

Publisher's Note to Readers of the *Family Therapy Collections*

Volume 25 marks the close of *Family Therapy Collections (FTC)* under the editorship of James C. Hansen. Dr. Hansen has thoughtfully orchestrated each of the volumes that comprise this series and nurtured the volume editors through the sometimes rocky publication process.

We are most grateful to Jim Hansen for his intelligent crafting of this series. The complete set will remain available to interested readers and a new set is being considered now although plans have not been finalized. If our readers have any suggestions regarding continuation of the *Collections*, please direct them to me at Aspen Publishers.

Dr. Hansen and the many contributors to the *Collections* have produced a fine compendium of perspectives and approaches in family therapy. We thank Dr. Hansen for seeing us through 25 volumes and wish him well in his life after *FTC*.

Margaret Quinlin
Editorial Director
March 1988

A Closing Note from the Series Editor

THE *FAMILY THERAPY COLLECTIONS* is a quarterly publication in which topics of current and specific interest to family therapists are presented. This is the final volume in the series under my editorship, and I would like to review the goals and accomplishments of the *Collections* during the past six years.

The *Collections* was conceived as a hard-back journal but actually came to be thought of more as a monograph series. It was designed to provide practical applications for practitioners by gathering, synthesizing, and applying the research and conceptual literature of the family therapy field. Each volume focused on a specific topic and was edited by a person recognized as a leader in that field of family therapy. Each volume editor selected authors who were knowledgeable writers and experienced practitioners to write articles on the specific areas of their expertise. The dedication of the volume editors—encouraging the individual authors and bringing the edited manuscripts to publication—has made this series successful.

The Editorial Board is composed of distinguished individuals representing a variety of disciplines. Their multidisciplinary perspective has greatly added to the breadth and richness of this series. I am also grateful to the members of the Editorial Board for their support and guidance.

The title, *Family Therapy Collections*, was selected because each volume was a collection of articles on a specific topic and the series was a collection of topics in family therapy. Twenty-five volumes will have been published in this *Collection* including this present volume. These volumes have covered topics on specific problems, populations, and practices. Problem-oriented topics included violence, death, school, work, divorce, eating disorders, and stress. Populations receiving attention were single parents, remarried families, women, young children, couples, and families with a handicapped member. Specific volumes that focused on practices included indirect approaches, diagnosis, stages in the process, integrating research and practice, and a cultural perspective in family therapy.

Each volume has presented case illustrations to demonstrate practical methods in working with specific problems and families. Overall, our goal has been to carve out meaningful clinical areas in need of elaboration and direct the writing of topics toward concerns of practicing therapists. We feel this series has successfully met its designated goals and hope our readers will agree.

James C. Hansen
March 1988

Series Preface

This volume concentrates on couples therapy within the context of the family. Family therapy generally begins with a presenting problem of a child and is at least conceptually framed as a family system problem. In the course of family therapy, specific attention may be given to the couple. The marital couple's behavior may involve other family members in roles that are crucial in maintaining the problem patterns. Couple behavior may show complementary or symmetrical patterns. Both patterns can produce relationships that couples report as satisfying; however, these patterns may also maintain serious maladaptive interactions for them or others in the system.

When therapy is focused on the couple, it may examine the problems of each of the partners but usually does not address the behavior of the children. The couple's problems are generally treated as separate entities rather than part of the larger system. Another model suggests that the problems of couples can best be understood and resolved by working within the context of their families of origin. The articles in this volume have been prepared to examine a variety of situations and illustrate many treatment modalities.

The volume editor is Florence Kaslow, an internationally known teacher, lecturer, therapist, author, and editor. She is presently in independent practice as a psychologist and mediator in West Palm Beach, Florida. She is also Director of the Florida Couples and Family Institute, an Adjunct Professor of Medical Psychology in the Department of Psychiatry at Duke University Medical School, and a Visiting Professor of Psychology at Florida Institute of Technology. Dr. Kaslow is past Editor of the *Journal of Marital and Family Therapy* and is currently on the editorial boards of *Journal of Marital and Family Therapy, Professional Psychology, Psychotherapy, Journal of Clinical Child Psychology,* and the *Journal of Family Psychology* among others. She has edited and/or co-authored twelve books and has over 75 articles published in professional journals. She received The Distinguished Family Psychologist of the Year

Award in 1986; in 1987 she became the first president of the International Family Therapy Association and was elected to the prestigious National Academies of Practice as a Distinguished Practitioner in Psychology.

Dr. Kaslow has selected outstanding authors who describe numerous couple relationships and offer examples of several approaches to therapy. This fine volume will serve for many years as a reference to therapists working with couples.

James C. Hansen
Series Editor

Preface

This volume was "invited" to focus on the couple in the context of the family rather than on the larger nuclear or extended family as the unit of treatment. In the field, emphasis on the family in the last few decades, the keystone of the family unit—the marital pair—has often been eclipsed as a dyadic unit that sometimes needs separate therapeutic attention. There are nonmarried, but deeply involved, couples who seek treatment in the (allegedly) safe sanctuary of the therapist's office. Seeking our assistance are couples in the pre-child stage of life, couples whose children are grown, as well as marital pairs who want to focus on adult issues without the presence of children.

Thus, we have attempted to create a volume that highlights some of the many kinds of problems, syndromes, symptoms, dynamics, and dysfunctional patterns seen by practicing clinicians in the 1980s. The systems aspects and the treatment modalities of single couples and couples group therapy are addressed. Most of the major theoretical schools of marital and family therapy, including integrative, are utilized since they constitute the underpinnings of the various authors' conceptualizations of the patient's reality and their interventive strategies.

Building on the extant literature, each author has tried to push the boundaries and explore some new terrain. Old areas of study have been revisited, and a new perspective presented. Some of the authors are senior and well respected members of the profession; others are more junior therapists who are doing exemplary work and have important observations and conclusions to convey from a fresh perspective.

Despite dire predictions about the future of marriage and the family, most people choose to live in dyadic, committed relationships—marital and non-marital—and the spiralling divorce rate has finally plateaued and may be reversing. Thus, it is imperative that we increase our knowledge about, understanding of, and skill in treating *COUPLES*, while always being mindful of their reciprocal impact on each other as individuals, and on all of their significant others.

Florence W. Kaslow
Volume Editor

Part I

Couples Therapy from Several Perspectives

1. Treating Couples in Group Therapy

Nadine J. Kaslow, PhD
Assistant Professor of Psychology in Psychiatry
Yale University School of Medicine
New Haven, Connecticut

Amado F. Suarez, MD
Assistant Professor of Psychiatry
Yale University School of Medicine
New Haven, Connecticut

Susan entered the room with her head down, tears in her eyes, and her body shaking. Mark, with whom she lives, was holding her up. Although Mark typically becomes histrionic under stress, he appeared relatively calm. Once seated, Susan maintained an almost catatonic state, unspeaking and unresponsive to others' concerns about her. During the session, Joan announced that she was furious with her husband, Charles, because he had a persistent case of pediculosis pubis (crabs) that he had acquired from a prostitute. Embarrassed at this revelation, Charles responded by threatening separation. Meanwhile, Estelle is feeling torn apart by the need to decide among various potentially dangerous medical treatments for her migraines and endometriosis. Her husband, Mario, spent the previous weekend in the country, seemingly oblivious to Estelle's distress.

Therapists find themselves immersed in a myriad of intrapsychic, dyadic, and group processes when working with a couples group. The basic theoretical framework of the group work described is that of object relations theory as it provides a bridge between the intrapsychic and interpersonal worlds (Slipp, 1984). The interventions utilized in the group are an integration of psychoanalytical, structural, family-of-origin, and behavioral techniques.

Individuals bring into their marital relationship problems that originated in their family of origin. Historically, such problems have been treated on an individual basis. It was not until 1942 that couples therapy was established, and couples group therapy is an even more recent phenomenon (Alger, 1976).

REVIEW OF RELEVANT LITERATURE

Research findings indicate that couples therapy is more effective than is individual therapy in treating marital distress (Gurman & Kniskern, 1981). Couples group therapy combines the healing ingredients of couples therapy with those of group therapy. The group:

- serves as a source of hope and universality
- provides a forum for information exchange in such areas as communicating, parenting, and socializing techniques
- offers an atmosphere that supports behavior change
- facilitates feedback from multiple perspectives, thereby increasing group cohesiveness
- provides a setting that allows participants to face existential issues (Grunebaum, 1986; Yalom, 1985).

Psychoanalytical, behavioral, and systems approaches have been adapted for couples group therapy. Markowitz and Kadis (1972) described a short-term, closed-ended analytical treatment of married couples in a group that focuses on helping individuals gain insight into the impact on their marital relationship of the intrapsychic difficulties that stem from their family-of-origin relationships. The male-female co-therapist dyad recaptures the nuclear situation, thus facilitating the development and resolution of parental transferences.

The open-ended couples groups described by Framo (1973) focus on the marital dyad and facilitate the differentiation of the partners from the marital symbiosis. Couples are encouraged to examine the "unwritten contract, a set of expectations and promises, conscious and unconscious" (Sager, 1976, p. ix) that each partner brought into the relationship. Like Markowitz and Kadis (1972), Framo used groups to help individuals understand the relationship between their unresolved conflicts with their family of origin and their current marital strife. This approach deemphasizes the group process, although the group process may be utilized to facilitate change.

Lieberman (Kaslow & Lieberman, 1981) described an open-ended couples group that is less structured and more focused on group process. He did not emphasize the dyad because of his concern that, in the group setting, each dyad would replay redundant and collusive interactional patterns, thereby tri-angulating the therapists and/or the group. Furthermore, the focus on the individual, rather than the couple, promotes healthy individuation that increases the capacity for intimacy.

The three models that have been detailed are based on psychodynamic theory. There is also a small body of literature on couples group therapy from a behavioral and social learning perspective (Jacobson & Margolin, 1979). Behavioral marital therapy is predicated on the assumption that the spouses are willing to work together to develop a more satisfying relationship. The role of insight is minimal, and transference phenomena receive little attention; instead, the therapist focuses on concrete, observable, and manipulatable contingencies of interpersonal reinforcement. Group behavioral therapy affords couples the opportunity to observe and learn from other participants' problem-solving and communication skills.

Papp (1976) described a 12-session approach to couples group therapy in which systemic and strategic interventions are utilized. The goal is to intervene in the presenting problem by effecting immediate and relevant behavior change through planned strategy. Family choreography, prescribed tasks, and a group setting are important components of this treatment.

THE GROUP SETTING

The community clinic in which the group discussed here receives therapy is a satellite clinic of a large community mental health center that is affiliated with a well-known medical school. Professionals in multiple mental health disciplines practice and train in this clinic, where there is a strong emphasis on family and group therapy. The town in which the clinic is located has 50,000 residents who are primarily lower middle class Italian Catholics. The population of the community is stable, and the integrity of the nuclear and extended family is highly valued. Couples group therapy was initiated in the clinic in 1984.

The primary impetus for the initiation of this approach at the clinic was the therapists' desire to work together in this modality. There were other consid-erations, however, such as the training and supervision that co-leadership of a group by a faculty member and a trainee affords, the fact that the group approach encourages an effective use of clinic resources (e.g., personnel, time, finances), and the provision of an additional modality of treatment for couples.

Several goals determine the way in which the therapists conduct treatment. First, the group approach is designed to facilitate more adaptive interpersonal behavior between partners by helping them to understand the interlocking nature of their relationship bond. Second, the group offers education and mirroring that supports the couples in modifying problematic dyadic patterns.

Third, group members accept, support, and identify with one another; as group cohesiveness evolves, members offer constructive criticism and evaluations of each other. Fourth, the therapists attend to each individual's intrapsychic dynamics, particularly focusing on unresolved conflicts that directly impinge on the marital relationship. Finally, they address family-of-origin and family-of-creation (one's spouse and children) difficulties in an effort to promote healthier family relationships.

SELECTION CRITERIA

Different authors have recommended various selection criteria for participants in couples group therapy. For example, Papp (1976) believed that the presenting complaints should be marital problems. Other recommended criteria include the couple's willingness to resolve their marital difficulties (Alger, 1976) and the existence of a basically sound marriage, which includes sexual exclusivity (Kaslow & Lieberman, 1981). Some authors (e.g., Kaslow, 1981; Lieberman & Lieberman, 1986), but not all, feel that outpatient couples group therapy is inappropriate for individuals with severe psychopathology, such as psychotic disorders, significant substance abuse, active suicidal or homicidal ideation, and severe personality disorders.

A number of authors emphasize the need for a considerable degree of homogeneity within the group. According to Leichter (1975), couples in a therapy group should be at similar stages of the life cycle. However, some heterogeneity regarding such variables as symptoms, socioeconomic status, education level and job status, ethnicity, and religion may enhance the group process (e.g., Lieberman & Lieberman, 1986).

The selection criteria for our couples group took into account those factors deemed important in the literature and the nature of the patient population in the clinic. Although the chief complaint was not always marital conflict, each couple acknowledged relationship difficulties as a significant concern and expressed a willingness to work on the relationship. A stable marriage was not a realistic admission criterion, because couples who have a basically healthy relationship do not generally seek treatment at a community mental health clinic. Although a certain degree of homogeneity may be desirable, we have developed a cohesive group that includes a couple in their 20s who are not married, but who have lived together for 6 years, and a couple in their 40s who have three children. We concur with those authors who exclude from the group individuals who evidence severe psychopathology; in addition, we exclude those who have organic brain syndromes or who are mentally retarded. We admit, however, individuals who are on psychotropic medications, as well as individuals with a past history of substance abuse and psychiatric hospitalizations.

STRUCTURE AND GROUND RULES

The couples group, which consists of three heterosexual couples and a heterosexual pair of co-therapists, meets one night per week for 75 minutes. Our experience is consistent with reports that the optimal group size is three or four couples (e.g., Alger, 1976). A group that includes fewer than three couples does not appear to provide a critical mass of dynamic material and inhibits the development of a therapeutic group process. A group that includes more than four couples, although recommended by some authors (e.g., Kaslow [1981], who will allow as many as five couples in a treatment group), does not seem to allow adequate time in a session to deal with each couple's critical issues.

Before a couple enters the group, a member of the clinic staff thoroughly evaluates the couple's problem. Then, the group leaders conduct an intake interview to ascertain the couple's appropriateness for the group. Additionally, the leaders discuss the nature and the purpose of the group with the couple and address the couple's initial anxieties.

Although the group was originally intended to last only one training year, the group members decided to redefine the group as open-ended. The therapists concurred, as the open-ended group affords the individuals the necessary time to work on significant interpersonal and intrapsychic issues. Therapists who work with such groups must remember, however, that long-term groups may foster an unrealistic dependence that may interfere with autonomous functioning in each individual and couple and may pose difficulties in confronting separation anxiety problems (Markowitz & Kadis, 1972).

While group membership is relatively stable, there are provisions to add couples when vacancies occur. There are advantages and disadvantages to a group model in which new members are added when old members leave. According to Lieberman's model (Kaslow & Lieberman, 1981), open-ended groups allow old members to take a strong, active role as they contribute support and guidance to newer members. Our experience indicates that new members contribute a new energy and a new perspective to the group. Kaslow (1981) observed that a time-limited closed group is more stable and allows members to develop trusting relationships with one another. Although a closed group may be ideal for short-term therapy, it may not be realistic for long-term therapy.

In starting any group, the therapists generally agree on some basic ground rules: confidentiality, regular and punctual attendance, and open and direct communication. There are differences in the implementation of these rules, however. We stress the importance of not discussing group material outside of the group except with one's significant other in privacy; but unlike Lieberman and Lieberman (1986), we allow the mention of specific names and places within group discussions. Because responsible attendance promotes a sense of consistency and dependability within the group (Kaslow, 1981), regular and punctual attendance is expected. Group members are asked to contact the therapists in advance to explain lateness and/or absence, as well as to inform the group of forthcoming absences.

Couples group therapists recognize that it is best to have both partners in attendance at group sessions. The expectation that both partners will attend underscores the fact that both partners must make a commitment to themselves, to their relationship, and to the group. It is our conviction that a significant proportion of couples who seek treatment have difficulties in these areas; therefore, an original ground rule for our group was that no individual could attend unless his or her spouse was present. The group members negotiated a change in this rule, however, arguing that they needed to attend the group even when their spouse could not. Most authors concur with our group members on the ground that individual attendance enables a focus on intrapsychic issues (Framo, 1973). Furthermore, as Alger (1976) remarked, a rule that excludes one partner if the other does not attend provides each partner with unfair power over the other. Our experience also suggests that, when individual attendance is permitted, the group can support an individual during times of stress (e.g., when the spouse is away on a business trip). The management of information revealed in the absence of some group members is a complex issue; our approach has been to encourage group members to inform those who could not attend of what transpired during their absence.

Couples group therapists differ on the appropriateness of allowing one partner to remain in the group when the other partner terminates. We concur with Markowitz and Kadis (1972), as well as with Kaslow (1981), who asserted that the dyadic interaction can be focal only when both members are present. Some authors, including Lieberman (Kaslow & Lieberman, 1981), have stressed the "principle of spousal independence," which emphasizes the autonomy of the individual within the dyad and thus does not grant one spouse the power to terminate the other's participation. Framo (1973) allowed one partner to attend after the other partner terminated, but noted that this rarely occurs.

The question of attendance is also relevant for the therapists. Consistent with our original position that both members of each couple needed to be present, we initially stated that there would be no session unless both therapists were present. Just as the group resisted the rule that both members of the couple must be present, they argued against the cancellation of a session when one therapist could not attend. After two experiences in which there was considerable acting out (e.g., extramarital sexual contact) during a week in which the group did not meet, we changed our position. Sessions conducted by only one of the therapists are useful in addressing the tendencies of group members to split the therapists into "good and available" versus "bad and abandoning," which is reminiscent of earlier experiences with their parents. This work may be more likely to occur during the absence of one of the therapists since group members may be more likely to share their feelings and fantasies about the absent and present therapist. Although Lieberman suggested that a leaderless group may be helpful to its members (Kaslow & Lieberman, 1981), our group does not appear to be developmentally prepared to function without the structure and guidance that the therapists provide.

Several authors (e.g., Alger, 1976; Framo, 1973) stressed the fact that open and direct communication is important to promote a good "holding environment" (Winnicott, 1965) in which individuals feel safe and respected. When discussing the ground rules, we place a premium on honest, forthright, and sensitive communication of thoughts and feelings. We inform members that the group cannot function effectively if partners engage in destructive communication at home as a result of the group process. We discourage acting out of impulses, yet encourage members to disclose acting out behaviors when they do occur (e.g., substance abuse, extramarital affairs). Some authors maintain that affairs during group therapy are unacceptable (Lieberman & Lieberman, 1986); while we agree that sexual exclusivity is an indicator of commitment to the relationship, some individuals in significant distress are likely to engage in affairs. Our expectation is that any such affairs are discussed, understood, and ultimately terminated. The one behavior that we prohibit is physical violence.

One of the most controversial ground rules concerns the acceptability of contact among group members outside group sessions. Lieberman and Lieberman (1986) discouraged outside socializing on the ground that extra-group socializing is often the first stage of subgrouping, which can have a disruptive effect on the course of the therapy group (Yalom, 1985). In contrast, Grunebaum (1986) supported extra-group socializing, provided that it is discussed in the group session, because he believed that peer relationships are vital to healthy development and are useful in correcting early and problematic peer experiences. Although we make it clear that we do not approve of extra-group contact, group members have sometimes initiated contact in times of stress. This has been discussed in the group session, and, although group members have been responsive to our interpretations of their behavior, they maintain that extra-group contact is supportive. For example, the other couples chose to attend the wake when one group member's mother died during the member's treatment.

While group members are encouraged to deal with couples issues in the group setting, the therapists are available to them at other times, particularly during times of extreme stress. Additionally, if group members need other forms of treatment (e.g., individual psychotherapy, psychopharmacological intervention), the group therapists have contact with other members of the treatment team. All outside contacts with the group therapists are acknowledged in the group. Furthermore, we urge group members to share relevant material that arises in other treatment contacts.

The final ground rule addresses termination. Couples are encouraged to have planned, rather than abrupt terminations. If they make a sudden decision to leave the group, they are requested to attend two additional sessions.

GROUP PROCESS

Stages of the Group

The functioning of our couples group has paralleled to some degree both the stages of a group delineated by Yalom (1985) in his work with groups of individuals and the multiple couples therapy described by Alger (1976). In the early stage, the group struggled with issues of orientation, dependency, and a search for meaning. Their erratic attendance and their assertions that external circumstances might make it impossible for them to remain in the group reflected the hesitancy of some couples to join the group. Although all members were seeking help, many were reluctant to share their problems with strangers because of their feelings of inadequacy about themselves and their marriage. These feelings conflicted with their need to share their pain in order to gain acceptance and support from the leaders and other group members. The resolution of this conflict was a particularly difficult task because only two of the three couples consistently attended the group sessions, while a number of "third" couples participated briefly in the group. After a few months, however, there was a stable group of three couples. The search for meaning was most apparent as couples identified the major problematic issues that they needed to address in the group: communication problems, difficulties with assertion and appropriate handling of anger, lack of respect and empathy within the dyad, problematic relationships with families of origin, and difficulties working together as effective parents.

Once the members developed a working alliance, the group entered the middle stage of treatment. Early in this stage, couples that had begun significant arguments outside the group often continued these arguments in the group. As they gained a greater understanding of the function of these arguments and learned skills that enabled them to fight more effectively, such arguments decreased in frequency and intensity. This stage was followed by a stage in which group members reported their progress, as evidenced by a decrease in depressive symptoms; improved job functioning; a new home or apartment, which sometimes entailed moving away from the family of origin; an increased feeling that their partner cares about them; and an increased capacity to have fun with their partner, including "dates" together. Following this period, the group members began to struggle with more painful and distressing issues, such as difficulties with intimacy, sexual problems, extramarital affairs, separation/individuation from their respective families of origin, and character/style problems.

During the later stages of couples group therapy, the members not only attain a capacity for both separateness and intimacy, but also are more able to negotiate their differences effectively. As group members confront termination issues, the therapists may note some regression. Couples may ask whether they can manage on their own. Our current group has not reached the last stage of treatment, despite the group's 1½-year existence. The reasons for this include the severity of the marital difficulties, the significant character pathology of each group member, the annual change of one of the therapists, and the recent introduction of a new couple.

Major Themes

Among the major themes that have surfaced during the course of our group are the role of each partner in a relationship, family of origin, intimacy, and loss. In respect to roles, couples may ask "Who is the captain of the ship?" and "Who is the sick partner, and who is the care-giver?" These concerns reflect the couples' dissatisfaction with the ways in which they have transferred their roles in their respective families of origin to their current relationship. In some cases, sociocultural factors (e.g., the women's movement) have forced the partners to redefine their roles. At the core of these struggles are issues of trust, competence, and power. The group establishes an environment in which couples work together in a trusting relationship, are mutually respectful of one another, acknowledge each other's strengths and weaknesses, and accept their differences. As a result, couples can make explicit their role definitions and expectations.

Our group members frequently address their difficulties with their family of origin and/or their spouse's family of origin by asking "Why aren't they more understanding of my needs?" "Why do I get so crazy when I am around them?" or "How can I develop a better relationship with them?" Unresolved family-of-origin issues are powerful influences on the intrapsychic and interpersonal worlds of the group members (Bowen, 1978). Each couple in our first group presented their genogram (family tree), which was then displayed during every session; these genograms facilitated family-of-origin work in which each individual developed an awareness of the patterns in his or her family as they affected the current life situation. Initially, each individual in the group constructed his or her genogram and subsequently each couple's genogram was integrated. While our current group has expressed an interest in sharing their genograms, every time we have initiated this work, at least one couple has presented a crisis. Interpretations of this pattern have been of no avail. Responses to these interpretations suggest that for both conscious and intentional reasons, as well as unconscious reasons, group members are reluctant to share in detail information about their families of origin. Group members are willing to discuss some of their difficulties with their families of origin, however. The goal of this work is not only to help members understand the relationship between patterns in their families of origin and their current marital situation, but also to develop more positive and accepting ways of relating to their family and to utilize insights gained in altering nonadaptive interpersonal behavior.

Our group members both desire and fear intimate relationships. They wonder aloud: "How can we be close without losing ourselves in the relationship?" "How can we develop a good sexual relationship?" "How can we develop other close relationships [nonsexual] that won't interfere with our relationship?" These queries indicate the nature and extent of our group members' conflicts regarding intimacy. Although the group initially resisted the discussion of sexual intimacy by bringing up a current concern or crisis, group members have become more trusting, and brief forays into the bedroom have been possible. Significant disagreements between spouses regarding the nature of their sexual contact have emerged. These discussions have been so painful that sexual contact outside the marital dyad and threats of separation have followed them. Sexual difficulties are symbolic of the couples' problems in negotiating intimacy within the relationship. It is hoped that, as the group process fosters individuation and ego integration, each person will develop a capacity for *intimacy without fusion*. As the partners feel more comfortable with themselves and with the relationship, they will feel freer to develop friendships and outside interests that can be integrated into the relationship.

Group members are encouraged to discuss losses (e.g., of group members, therapists, family members, marital bonds) and the related feelings in order to understand how these losses affect their current relationship. All participants are concerned that, if they share their thoughts and feelings, they risk alienating—or even losing—significant people in their life. These fears may reflect unresolved feelings of abandonment and rejection in the past. Additionally, these fears may be an expression of a group process in which the group attempts to avoid the expression of conflict and negative feelings. The aim of therapy in this area is to help group members identify the feelings that surround the losses in their life and learn adaptive coping mechanisms so that these experiences do not interfere with healthy intrapsychic and interpersonal functioning.

The transference issues that have emerged during the course of therapy reflect the aforementioned themes. The group has struggled with questions such as who is the more powerful and/or more competent therapist (e.g., faculty member versus trainee, male versus female, M.D. versus Ph.D.). Because of the presence of the heterosexual co-therapy dyad, the group members develop parental transferences reminiscent of family-of-origin relationships. The conflicts of group members regarding intimacy are evident in their relationships with the therapists as they test the boundaries of the therapeutic relationship (e.g., by making frequent telephone calls during stressful times), as well as in their questions regarding the nature of the co-therapists' relationship (e.g., whether they are a couple). Finally, group participants experience termination of therapy as an event similar to early childhood losses, and it is essential for the group to help members process the meaning of this loss vis-à-vis their current relationships. The group members find it easier to work through this transference material when they are led by a competent male-female co-therapy team who have developed a solid working alliance. Such a co-therapy team models both effective parenting and a realistic, positive partnership.

CONCLUSION

Couples group therapy is an effective and efficient modality for working with couples in distress. Conducting a couples group can be an extremely positive experience for therapists as they witness the significant progress that each individual and dyad makes. As the group matures, members are more willing to work with issues of greater significance and to function as a support system for one another. While group sessions can be very intense at times, therapists and group members can also enjoy periods of playfulness and creativity.

REFERENCES

Alger, I. (1976). Multiple couple therapy. In P. Guerin (Ed.), *Family therapy: Theory and practice* (pp. 364–387). New York: Gardner.

Bowen, M. (1978). *Family therapy and clinical practice.* New York: Jason Aronson.

Framo, J.L. (1973). Marriage therapy in a couples group. In D. Block (Ed.), *Techniques of family psychotherapy: A primer* (pp. 87–97). New York: Grune & Stratton.

Grunebaum, H. (1986). Inside the group. In A.S. Gurman (Ed.), *Casebook of marital therapy* (pp. 73–95). New York: Guilford Press.

Gurman, A.S., & Kniskern, D.P. (1981). Family therapy outcome research: Knowns and unknowns. In A.S. Gurman & D.P. Kniskern (Eds.), *Handbook of family therapy* (pp. 742–775). New York: Brunner/Mazel.

Jacobson, N.S., & Margolin, G. (1979). *Marital therapy: Exchange principles.* New York: Brunner/Mazel.

Kaslow, F.W. (1981). Group therapy with couples in conflict: Is more better? *Psychotherapy: Theory, Research and Practice, 18,* 516–524.

Kaslow, F., & Lieberman, E.J. (1981). Couples group therapy: Rationale, dynamics, and process. In G.P. Sholevar (Ed.), *The handbook of marriage and marital therapy* (pp. 347–362). New York: S.P. Medical and Scientific Books.

Leichter, E. (1975). Treatment of married couples groups. In A.S. Gurman & D.G. Rice (Eds.), *Couples in conflict* (pp. 175–191). New York: Jason Aronson.

Lieberman, E.J., & Lieberman, S.B. (1986). Couples group therapy. In N. Jacobson & A. Gurman (Eds.), *Clinical handbook of marital therapy* (pp. 237–251). New York: Guilford Press.

Markowitz, M., & Kadis, A.L. (1972). Short-term analytic treatment of married couples in a group by a therapist couple. In C. Sager & H.S. Kaplan (Eds.), *Progress in group and family therapy* (pp. 463–482). New York: Brunner/Mazel.

Papp, P. (1976). Brief therapy with couples groups. In P.J. Guerin (Ed.), *Family therapy: Theory and practice* (pp. 350–363). New York: Gardner Press.

Sager, C.J. (1976). *Marriage contracts and couple therapy.* New York: Brunner/Mazel.

Slipp, S. (1984). *Object relations: A dynamic bridge between individual and family treatment.* New York: Jason Aronson.

Winnicott, D.W. (1965). *The maturational processes and the facilitating environment.* London: Hogarth Press and the Institute of Psychoanalysis.

Yalom, I.D. (1985). *The theory and practice of group psychotherapy* (3rd ed.). New York: Basic Books.

2. Dealing with Divorce in a Country that Has Only Recently Started to Recognize Divorce

Carlos Maria Diaz Usandivaras, MD
Co-Director of the Psychological Assistance Teaching and Research Center
Co-Director of Counseling—Counseling Center for
Families Affected by Marital Breakup
Professor of Family Psychology
University of Buenos Aires Law School
President, Divorcing Process Families and Remarriage
of the Argentine Family Therapy Society
Buenos Aires, Argentina

I n countries with rapidly developing social structures, social changes are typically asynchronal. Thus, some social features may change, while others remain intact. Generally this "no change" hides behind the rules and the social system's dictates whenever reality shows a deviation. This conflict may lead to symptomatic or painful situations if, once reality imposes its changes on society, rules do not adjust to the times.

One of the asynchronal processes in the social structures is the incongruence between (1) the social and legal rules that govern couples and families, and (2) the actual behaviors when faced with marital breakdown in a developing and socially changing country such as Argentina, where there is no possibility for legally dissolving wedlock. The consequences of this incongruence on the legal, social, and psychological treatment of the divorced couple and family and their different support systems can be devastating.

Troubled Argentine couples who cannot resolve their difficulties through therapy frequently exchange the services of a therapist for those of a lawyer. Years later, these families may need counseling (e.g., because of a symptomatic child or teen-ager), almost always as a result of the previous process, which had taken place out of my reach: The Evil Divorce. Then, when it was already too late, I found the serious consequences of poorly handled divorced families. Just like the pathologist who does an autopsy and explains—too late—why the patient died, how the patient died, and which medical decisions were right and which were not, therapists may find themselves participating in "family autopsies." It seems that the only possible way to avoid these subsequent problems is for therapists to continue providing therapy throughout the process of marital dissolution. It is necessary, therefore, for Argentine therapists (1) to know the legal divorce system and the law, (2) to interact with lawyers and other legal personnel, and (3) to deal with couples at different stages of the divorce process.

The most important members of the Argentine community, whose opinions are public and influential, as well as the lawyers and mental health specialists (who usually act as consultants), have continued to subscribe to the old rules pertaining to divorce. They approach the subject, almost always, from an individual and linear epistemology, even though today it is known that human behavior is better understood by means of a holistic approach and the framework of circular causality. Now, however, Argentina is facing an important change. Not satisfied with the present situation, law and mental health professionals and legislators are beginning to establish interdisciplinary teams to help Argentine society change its rules, particularly those dealing with civil matrimony and psychosocial assistance to divorcing families. A systemic approach, along with holistic concepts and a circular causality perspective, turn out to be a more effective approach in terms of explaining and solving these problems. This could modify the work of courts and support systems.

SOCIAL SYSTEM RULES

Argentina, like most Latin American countries, has a Latin, Luso-Spanish heritage based on the most conservative Catholic standards. These traditions make up the social norms that, in regard to marriage and divorce, lead to two basic conditions: (1) the *macho-matriarchal bias* and (2) sexual repression.

A great deal has been said about the macho attitude, but a linear thinking process has resulted in the underestimation of its counterpart, the matriarchal bias. According to these two concepts, men are owners of the outside world (e.g., money, work, and sex). In contrast, women are the owners of the household (e.g., children, their education, and their introduction to culture and mores). These are the two sides of a tacit agreement in Argentine society, a "Quid pro Quo," not always taken into account. This bias makes man the "guilty" party in all marital crises. It implies the possibility that, guilty or not, the man goes on to another partner. It establishes his ownership of the possessions acquired through "his work" and his importance to the family only as supplier, not as a functional parent. The woman, on the other hand, is considered the "victim" of divorce. Her maternal role precedes her sexual one and, therefore, it is widely believed that a divorced woman must choose her children as partners because her sexual role endangers her functioning as a parent. Children are "her" undeniable possession because she has "borne and raised them" and only she is important to their welfare and education, at least in terms of personal relationships. The postdivorce division tends to apply the same bias, allowing the man to keep "his" money and the possibility of remarrying, but without his children. The woman usually has to devote herself to "her" children, who constitute "her property." This excludes the father from the relationship. She then lacks both economically, since he provides no support, and sexually, as she is to be faithful to her maternal role.

Argentine society considers matrimony the only acceptable context for the expression of sexuality, and procreation its only reason. Generally, this prejudice blames divorce on sexual "sins," almost always attributable to men's polygamous tendencies. This position undervalues a woman's sexuality and ignores the fact that nonsexual causes may estrange a couple. This creates the image of a person who is not satisfied with his or her partner's sexuality and sets out to look for a new mate, abusing a right that has to be restricted. The spouse seeking divorce is, then, taking advantage of the situation and not at all unhappy because of the marital breakdown. The situation narrows down to a guilty party and an innocent party, a sinner and a victim, a good spouse who is able to raise children and to denounce sexuality and a bad spouse who should be kept away from the children. Any attempted remarriage is deemed a sinful, invalid relationship, a mere "concubinage." This is the approach taken in the Canonical Code, the original source of Argentine matrimony laws.

Many social trends, opinions, myths, and attitudes are strongly influenced by these prejudices. Furthermore, many Argentine laws are written under these concepts and designed to preserve them. Finally, as may be expected, many mental health professionals still adhere to these biases.

LEGAL SYSTEM RULES

> We assume that laws are means to achieve certain goals, based on strategies or realities, confirmed by experience, technically or scientifically, in force when passed. Even if we consider those goals as permanent, we must accept that strategies, useful at a given moment, may turn out not to be so in a different moment. In other words, time may render law inadequate as a means to reach the desired aim: in this case, the welfare and strength of the family unit and its role in children['s] socialization. (Diaz Usandivaras, 1986)

Except for some changes issued in 1968, the law in Argentina today remains largely as it was written in 1869. In those days, the Argentine Civil Code was an exemplary, modern code of laws, as can be seen, for example, in Article 213 on the effects of divorce:

> Children under five will always remain with the mother. Children beyond that age will be given to the spouse who, according to the judge, is best for their education. Neither spouse has a preferential right to keep the children.

This law was based on the assumption that it is possible to be simultaneously a bad spouse and a good parent, dissociating the marital and parental functions. Unfortunately, 100 years later in 1968, this law was changed. The new legislation yielded certain improvements, but it lost its advanced concept. The law now reads:

> Except for serious cases, children under five will remain with the mother. Children beyond that age will remain with the innocent spouse, unless this solution should not be convenient for the child. If both spouses are guilty, the judge will choose the most convenient arrangement for the children. (Zavalia, 1986)

In this new law, marital and parental functions are mixed. The linear concept of guilt and innocence prevails, and children are used to reward the innocent and punish the guilty. This is clearly an instance in which the rules have been pushed backward instead of adjusted to reality. As Zavalia (1986) noted,

> In almost all Codes, the spouse who has caused divorce is denied the right to keep the children. According to the laws, children are to remain with the innocent spouse, whether he/she is able to raise and educate them or not. The relationship between husband and wife is not connected to the probable behavior of each with their children. I believe that children and the right to keep them cannot be used as punishment to the spouse causing divorce, that children's welfare should be the only consideration in dealing with parents' personal separation. (Zavalia, 1986)

Thus, under current Argentine law, divorce is a sanction for the spouse who commits certain transgressions and is, therefore, guilty. This criterion not only punishes the "guilty" parent, but also endangers his or her image in front of the children. It also helps the "innocent" parent avoid his or her share of the responsibility for the marital breakdown. Furthermore, this approach hinders the children's right to have a respectable and worthy image of both parents.

The breach of the marital contract, even if called "divorce," does not imply a breach in wedlock, which is considered undissolvable. Hence, it does not allow for remarriage. This is not, then, a true divorce. Fidelity is still compulsory according to the law and, consequently, any relationship with another partner becomes a violation to that mandatory fidelity, constituting adultery. If a new stable relationship is established, it is adulterous and its legal status is that of guilty concubinage, which can be held against the party in any lawsuit at the judge's discretion. So far, all attempts to amend the new law in a way that permits the dissolution of wedlock have failed. A new bill, providing for the possibility of true divorce and remarriage has been submitted to Congress, but it has not yet been passed. In the meantime, Argentinians are bound to the current law; even if the new bill is passed, they will suffer the consequences of the current law for quite some time to come.

In 1968, the Argentine Congress passed an amendment that allows the joint filing of a mutual consent divorce application of both spouses, but only on the grounds of severe causes. Mutual consent or desire to divorce is not enough. In this case, both spouses are considered guilty of failing to keep their marriage. Because the law does not require an agreement between the spouses on certain basic issues such as distribution of possessions, child custody, shared housing, alimony, and visiting rights before the divorce requested in such an application is granted (Wagmaister et al., 1986), a long series of disputes about these subjects often keeps the divorced couple "together" after the divorce. Furthermore, the law specifies that the common dwelling should not be divided so as to ensure housing stability for the offspring. This undoubtedly well-intentioned demand usually victimizes those it is actually trying to protect—the children—by requiring them to remain in an atmosphere of tension.

In Argentina, there are few special courts for family matters. Divorce cases and related incidents are handled by civil courts, which intersperse decisions on family issues with those on contracts, indemnities, and property titles. A judge, for example, may divide his time between a lawsuit for a violation of a contract and another for a father's visitation rights. A bill to establish family courts that could provide specialized attention for issues of family law has been submitted to Congress for approval.

An in-depth analysis of Argentina's civil matrimony law reveals that it is conceived from an individual epistemology. In other words, it views the family as the sum of the individual members. It zeroes in on the rights of the individual as the nucleus of rights and obligations, and not on the family as a whole. It seeks to recognize individual rights, ignoring the rights and needs of the family as a whole. Moreover, for the sake of one member, the law may jeopardize all members. Family law, therefore, is part of private law, which deals with citizens' individual and personal affairs.

Argentine law is organized in such a way as almost to guarantee an adversarial divorce process, in which the struggle between the parties is intense. There is little opportunity for a friendly and harmonious divorce, in which the spouses speak up, reach agreements, and treat each other with respect. The law provides the couple with a battleground rather than a negotiating table. This has created the worst possible conditions for the couple's postdivorce relationship. Although the law attempts to protect the children, it is useless to protect the children if their parents are harrassed. The law is the formal embodiment of the social rules. As long as social rules are biased, laws will adhere to these prejudices.

THE REAL SITUATION

The couple model based on the macho-matriarchal bias is less common today because women are no longer limited to the roles of housewife and mother. They are gradually acquiring a position that is more symmetrical to that of men, particularly in two significant areas: work and sexual expression. After sharing the outside world with women, men are more willing to share the household responsibilities, to take an active role in family decision making and in the education of the children, and to communicate their feelings.

When modern couples decide to divorce, these differences defy the macho-matriarchal bias and rules. No longer are the husbands the only ones to ask for divorce, nor are they the only ones interested in a second marriage. Today, women do not always prefer their role as mother to their role as wife, and they are not so willing to take full responsibility for the children with only limited economic assistance from their former husbands. Fathers do not so readily agree to leave their children, and they often fight to continue participating in their children's upbringing.

In spite of the stigma attached to second marriages in Argentina, there are now many formally remarried couples. Therefore, many children now live in binuclear families.

CONSEQUENCES

Legal Aspects

Because a strict application of the law is often unfair and unrelated to reality, judges must frequently resort to their own creativity and common sense in order to reach their decisions. The ultimate example of the incongruence that may result from this approach is a recent opinion of the Supreme Court of Justice, the highest court in Argentina; the Court stated in this opinion that the law forbidding divorced citizens to remarry stands as a limitation of a constitutional right and, thus, ruled that the plaintiff could remarry. Naturally, this ruling set a very significant and troublesome precedent, pressing Congress to deal promptly with the proposed new civil matrimony law that allows the dissolution of wedlock.

To complicate matters further, leaving the interpretation of ambiguous and unreliable laws to each judge's subjective judgment yields contradictory rulings, such as the following:

> The fact that the mother lives with a stranger [she was actually remarried] sets a harmful example for the daughter and makes it necessary to give her permanent custody to the father. However, since the father cannot personally take care of the child because of his work, she should be registered in an appropriate boarding school. (*La Ley*, 1981, 116–803)

> Since, from the virtual separation up to the present, the mother has taken care of the child, now twelve years old, and it has been found that the child has received proper education and he has expressed his wish to remain with her, there is no sense in taking the child away and forcing him to live in a different atmosphere where he does not want to go. The mother's second marriage abroad does not affect this decision because, for the child, it is a normal procedure and, hence, does not constitute a harmful example, considering the mother's good private behavior and her observance of maternal duties. Although a divorce and a second marriage carried out abroad is questionable for our laws, this sole evidence does not make her a dishonest and unable mother for her child's education. (Civil Court, Room F, August 13, 1959)

These two paragraphs seem to indicate that the decisions were based on different laws; in truth, however, only the judges' criteria differed.

Social Aspects

As a result of the conflict produced by rules that stress marriage continuity at all costs, condemn divorce, and even more emphatically condemn remarriage, many hopelessly troubled couples feel compelled to remain together. They argue that they live together for the sake of the children, although the children are actually damaged by the triangle (of parents and child) created to keep the system's balance. When a couple does divorce, the conflict with the rules may mean that any remarriage exists in semisecrecy and/or without respectability.

Alone and without resources, the mother is often driven to her family of origin during the postdivorce period. She places her maternal role before her sexual role, becoming overinvolved with her children and jeopardizing everyone's development. The fact that their father is no longer considered important hinders the children's relationship with him, and he may decide to abandon parenthood. Not always reasonably, women adopt the role of "victim." Finally, the prevailing laws have allowed social systems, such as schools, to look for problems in children whose parents have divorced, sometimes generating truly self-fulfilling prophecies.

Psychological Aspects

The rules condemning divorce suggest that all subsequent psychological problems result from the trauma that divorce entails and fail to take into account the pathogenic significance of dysfunctional postdivorce family organization. This somewhat fatalistic approach fails to help families, because it is based on a perception of the divorced family as a system that is sick, rather than as a system that is in rapid transition. Diagnosis and mental health reports are overvalued. Observation focuses on individuals and their inner psychological conflicts as they are related to the past, rather than to the present or to the future. Within this approach, individual therapy is usually recommended. Family ties are perceived as essentially dyadic, centered in mother-child symbiosis, with little recognition and psychological significance awarded to the mother-child-father triad. Actually, it is impossible for a family to go through divorce as a normal family process in Argentina or in any other country where divorce is forbidden or severely stigmatized.

NEW EXPERIENCES

The unsatisfactory effects of the legal, social, and psychological incongruencies between the law and reality drove therapists, lawyers, social workers, judges, congressional representatives, and other community leaders to get together in order to establish common standards for thought and action. From criticisms of the consequences alluded to above, a different concept of the problem arose, reached on the basis of an interactive point of view.

- family law should be a special branch of laws, with a place and a purpose of its own
- the family as a whole unit is more important than the sum of the individual members
- family cases should be handled in special courts, not in civil courts

Therefore, these professionals are now "fighting for" the creation of family courts.

It is essential to abolish the ambiguous legal entity of a divorce that is not a divorce so that remarriage can become a respectable, useful, and healthy feature of social organization. As Goldsmith (1980) stated, "The post-divorce family system still involves the same members, although their attributes and the relationship between them have changed. The family system is not dissolved, only altered." Therefore, the law on divorce should address not a broken family, but a family in the midst of a change process. The law, accordingly, should focus on the continuation of future co-parental relations and respect for the integrity and dignity of both parents in the eyes of their children.

In order to accept this approach, Argentine lawyers must undergo an epistemological and professional change, for they have been accustomed to working on the basis of past events, solid evidence, and the beliefs that total objectivity is possible and that justice is expressed in terms of guilt and innocence, no matter what the consequences of the verdict. For the past 3 years, therefore, efforts have been made to achieve this change in the thinking of family law specialists. The University of Buenos Aires Law School now offers a 2-year postgraduate course on family law that includes equal attention to family legal, social, and psychological issues. As a result, Argentine lawyers now take part in interdisciplinary teams to mediate family disputes and even to act as therapists. Above all, they have developed a constructive approach to divorce.

Interdisciplinary Approach

It is necessary to replace the patronizing attitude toward women and children that comes from the perception of a couple as a rigid complementary unit with a respectful attitude that arises from a more symmetrical outlook and fosters the development of all family members. Children should be repositioned as subjects with inherent rights instead of objects for the parents to fight over as they fight over shared property. In the matter of visitation rights, for example, those who adhere to the old approach try to guarantee the right of a parent to visit the child; however, those who adhere to the new approach are more interested in the child's right to keep a close postdivorce relationship with both parents. The ideal solution is shared custody, unless either parent is truly incapable. In cases of family law, the judge should not overrule the desires of the parents, except in extreme cases. A good family judge can promote agreement between the parties, making it unnecessary for the judge to rule on their behalf.

The individualistic approach allows the spouses to decide whether they will seek a supportive or mediating system to help them with their problem on the ground that making professional assistance compulsory would violate their individual freedom. If professional assistance is necessary for the entire family, however, such a decision should not be left to only some members. The judge can and, in fact, should insist on it, especially for the sake of the weaker members, to ensure that the family gets adequate help.

Interdisciplinary teams that include not only family therapists, but also representatives of the court and the parties' lawyers, should assist the divorcing family or couple. They should not deal with the psychological conflicts of each member of the family system; instead, they should focus on family relationships, concentrating on postdivorce family organization and hierarchical structure. Because behavior is complementary and reciprocal, determined by the family's current circumstances more than by the personal or historical characteristics of each family member, it seems certain that people can change if their circumstances do. Kaslow (1986) stated that when children and parents stay close to each other, through co-parenting arrangements, the feeling of disruption, loss, and abandonment is minimal.

During the crisis of divorce, many spouses can develop extreme, violent, psychotic, or incongruent behaviors; once the crisis has been resolved, however, effective support allows these people to recover their respectability, coherence, and sanity. Therefore, we are fighting against their being judged by their behavior at the time of divorce. This perception of human behavior as dynamic and changing does not allow therapists to use individual assessment techniques based on rigid principles about "personality," as if personality were static.

Work on the triadic family concept stresses the relationship of the child with both parents, upgrading the father's role. When the absent father reenters the mother-child dyadic system, the mother recovers her ability to relate to the outside world (e.g., work, sexuality), which she must leave behind in a symbiotic attachment to the child. In turn, the child begins to grow; parental functions, until then exclusively nurturing, start to include normative attitudes that enable the child to develop with more realistic principles.

Interdisciplinary assistance takes place at two basic levels:

1. The wide system structure made up of the divorcing spouses, their lawyers, sometimes their individual therapists, friends, extended families, court officials, and an interdisciplinary team. This evolves within the norms of society and the law.
2. The specific task of mediation or therapy carried out by the interdisciplinary team members within that structural framework.

It is necessary to restore coherence in the wide system, especially in terms of hierarchy, frontiers, relationships between different subsystems, and the correction of distorted interpretations of ambiguous laws and rules (Haley, 1967, 1976, 1980; Madanes, 1981). The mediating task requires an orderly approach and honest communication. Just as parental disagreement in front of a child automatically traps the child in an alliance with one of the parents or in an evil triangle, thus inevitably producing some damage (Haley, 1967, 1976), secret contacts, partial opinions, or disagreements between the team and the court undermine the effectiveness of efforts to provide assistance. The task is easier when all participants reach an "adult agreement"—together in front of the divorcing spouses. This leaves the spouses alone in their regressive position, deprived of willing or unwilling accomplices, and makes it absolutely necessary for both to cooperate.

At the beginning, the court is an important subsystem because of its authority to order professional assistance for a divorcing couple. It is still uncommon for spouses to seek help spontaneously; their participation is more likely to be a compliance, explicit or implicit, with a judge's requirement than a personal choice. The court is also important as the initial basis of the mediating team's neutral image. As the process develops, trust increases and the mediator's professional qualities and abilities increase. By reaching agreement, the couple gradually recapture the decision-making power that they lost to the judge during the lawsuit. Thus, the court's authority declines in importance until it finally becomes only the representation of justice, which ratifies the agreements reached by the spouses. Like therapists, judges have succeeded when they have made themselves unnecessary by helping families to solve problems, find new alternatives, and cope adequately with changing circumstances.

The process of "demedicalization" has proved fundamental to the interdisciplinary approach. Social, legal, and even therapeutic rules have condemned divorce, explicitly or implicitly, as pathological. Divorced people have been described as "not completely sane" or "subject to certain disorders." Psychiatrists and psychologists frequently confirm this construction of reality in their use and abuse of farfetched and unnecessary psychiatric nosological diagnoses. It is essential to reduce the perceptions caused by the participation of mental health professionals in the divorce process and to handle a divorce as something natural, even though it is a crisis that can be very painful. For that reason, therapists should try to avoid the frequent psychiatric or psychological investigations that medicalize the situation and often become another form of harassment to the parties, especially to children.

The first obstacle that mediators must face is a couple's lack of knowledge about or confidence in the interdisciplinary approach to divorce. The first step is to demonstrate neutrality regarding both parties, avoiding premature single interviews and partial contacts. Then, it is necessary to overcome the distrust between former spouses that creates a persecuting and uncommunicative atmosphere. Open dialogue helps to eliminate uncertainty and inaccurate references to certain issues, such as real income, a new relationship, or any other information that one of the parties can use to damage the other. Hence, the basic strategy is (1) to stop any negative interactive loop in which violence and contradiction prevail, and (2) to transform a competitive relationship into a cooperative one.

The most frequent problem centers on the visiting rights of the parent who does not have custody of the children. Generally, the mother is the custodial parent, and she may refuse to comply with the previously arranged visitation procedures on some ground or in some subtle and implicit way. Now, the father usually objects and strives to maintain his relationship with his children. Not so long ago, fathers abandoned their relationship with their children when faced with such obstacles—a situation that was unwittingly aided by legal procedures. Nowadays, many judges believe that father-child relationships are as important as mother-child relationships, and they try to defend the children's right to be involved with both parents.

Case Example

Jose, aged 36, had divorced Ana 5 years ago. Now, their 7-year-old daughter, Victoria, did not want to see her father. Jose blamed this rejection on Ana, claiming that she had given Victoria a distorted image of her father. Ana denied this, arguing that the child's attitude was in response to her father's inconsistency in their relationship. They had taken the issue to court, and the judge wanted a psychiatrist to determine why Victoria did not want to see her father and which visiting arrangement would be best.

Jose and Ana had obtained a mutual consent divorce and had signed an agreement giving custody of Victoria, then 2 years old, to her mother. The joint ownership of property had been terminated. Although the former family home belonged exclusively to Jose, it had been agreed that Ana could live there until Victoria came of age. This benefit would automatically end if Ana should establish a new couple. Alimony and visiting rights for the father had been settled. When Victoria refused to see him, Jose had filed a claim for his ex-wife's failure to comply with the agreed upon visiting arrangement.

Stating that Victoria's refusal to see her father was caused by her mother, Jose's lawyer threatened to demand that the child's custody be transferred to her father. We explained to the lawyer our belief that lawyers, judges, or courts could not resolve this case and suggested that we work with the couple in an effort to produce a change in the girl's attitude. Although he had expected to find some kind of sick relationship between mother and child that he could use on his client's behalf and was surprised at this very different approach, Jose's lawyer agreed. Ana's lawyer was also interested in our participation, as she is a family law specialist who considers interdisciplinary work very helpful in this type of situation. Thus, with the approval and support of both lawyers, we began work with the couple.

At the first session, Jose looked annoyed and distrusting. Ana futilely tried to convince him that she did not influence Victoria at all and that the child's attitude was probably a reaction to his behavior. The lack of communication between them was striking. Jose feared that Ana would find out about his new relationship and his improved economic situation. Ana did not know Jose's telephone number and could not keep him informed of important events in Victoria's life until he called. Once they realized that this lack of communication was harmful to Victoria, they started to come to terms with each other. Jose found that there was no need to hide information from Ana, because she already knew a great deal about him and, so far, this knowledge had not had any negative consequences. Ana finally admitted that it was her daughter's right to have a father. When their dialogue improved, they understood that Victoria's attitude toward her father was a direct result of the tense, competitive relationship between them. It was agreed to leave the issue of visits aside for a while and to focus on Victoria's well-being.

In that first interview, the parents were given two assignments: (1) to meet briefly every week and share their views on Victoria's upbringing and her welfare, and (2) to visit her school together and talk to her teacher about the child's behavior. Two weeks later, they reported that they had met twice, had avoided any references to the past, and had settled some outstanding issues about Victoria. The visit to Victoria's school was also a satisfactory experience; the teacher was also divorced, and she understood them fully, promised to help Victoria, and praised their attitude. Victoria had no severe problems at school, but the visit was good practice in co-parenthood. In addition, it was an important event for Victoria, as the teacher told her about it.

In the following interviews, which took place twice a month, we worked on their disputes. We suggested that Victoria would not accept Jose unless Ana accepted him as her co-parent with whom she had to share responsibilities. We asked them to continue meeting weekly to discuss issues that involved Victoria, letting her know about it but making it clear that those meetings did not indicate a reconciliation.

It became clear that Victoria rejected her father because of a loyalty conflict. Ana had always played the role of victim of Jose's desertion, behaving in a weak, helpless manner and crying easily when disturbed. Jose appeared to be the victimizer, strong and insensitive. Although he almost always behaved like a good father with Victoria, Ana had not been able to discriminate Jose's marital behavior, which obviously did not please her at all, from his parental behavior, which was satisfactory; she had considered him both a bad husband and a bad father. Feeling deserted, too, Victoria had taken her mother's side. Thus, a triangle had been established (Haley, 1967).

We helped Jose and Ana achieve a respectful and kind relationship, developing their ability to detect and avoid those situations that could trigger a violent or unpleasant reaction in the other, as well as to shun retaliation if such a situation did occur. It was also necessary to help them understand the importance of the father figure to a child, thus eradicating the matriarchal prejudice that the child needed only her mother's contact and love. This concept was redefined as unfair to Ana, since it forced her to take on the double responsibility of both mother and father roles. Jose and Ana began to realize that Victoria needed a responsible father with whom to share her time and affection.

During individual interviews, I dealt with areas in Ana's life that did not relate to her parental role, such as the possibility of starting a new emotional relationship. She had set this idea aside in order to abide by the original agreement that allowed her to remain in the family home only as long as she did not begin a new relationship. We talked about how unfair and paralyzing this agreement was for her own personal development. She developed more self-confidence and accepted the fact that she needed to share her daughter with Jose. While Ana and Jose compromised and agreed on the best course of action for their daughter, the court had become irrelevant, a mere spectator and the eventual ratifier of their decisions. We explained the new developments in this case to both lawyers and to the judge. Our own team lawyer proved to be very useful in this effort. This was a critical event for the whole system, because a mishandling of the legal subsystem could have led the court to reenter the dispute.

In spite of the progress that her parents had made, Victoria persisted in her refusal to see her father. We studied closely the family's attitudes when Jose tried to visit Victoria. Jose was firm about the appointment, but Ana was not. Actually, Ana simply allowed the child to decide whether she wanted to go with her father. In fact, it seemed that Ana gave Victoria an important share of everyday decisions, which leveled the mother-child hierarchy. Beyond Victoria's troubled relationship with her father and the problems that the parents had overcome, Victoria was now defending her powerful position in the family structure. If she agreed to see her father and resume the father-child relationship, she would break her alliance with her mother and consolidate her parents' joint position. Therefore, she would lose power, and she would have to accept her parents' authority.

It was necessary to help Ana reestablish the generational boundary and her decision-making authority. Although initially reluctant to do so, Ana finally told Victoria that she also wanted her to see Jose; this deprived Victoria of the choice. Firmly, Ana insisted that Victoria go with her father, in spite of the girl's protests. Gradually, Victoria established a natural and satisfactory relationship with her father. Of course, she displayed an expected negative reaction toward her mother for having broken the alliance, but Ana had been trained to handle this effectively and promptly. A month later, Jose dropped his court claim.

In this case, the most meaningful feature was the change in approach produced at different levels:

1. An emotional and psychotherapeutic process replaced the legal procedure.
2. A search for agreement between the spouses to rebuild relationships and recover parental authority replaced a legal tendency to look for guilty parties.
3. A mediating or therapeutic process that modified present and future events not only replaced the legal investigation intended to report or provide evidence of past events so as to help the judge reach a decision, but also rendered the judge's ruling unnecessary.

4. An interdisciplinary system that included the family, the court, both lawyers, and the therapists replaced the individual approach that centered on a diagnostic evaluation of the child.
5. An efficient co-parental relationship replaced the quest for the fulfillment of the father's visiting right.

These events made it possible to avoid a fruitless, repetitive task for the court and to prevent future conflicts within the family.

In Argentina, the lawyers, judges, and therapists who think and work along these interdisciplinary lines are still in the minority, but the number is increasing. These professionals can effect change in the social and legal rules of Argentina, as well as in the methods used to help divorced families during the crucial moments of transition.

EDITORIAL POSTSCRIPT

The article by Dr. Diaz Usandivaras illustrates the myriad problems encountered by couples who seek to divorce and remarry in countries where it is forbidden. (In almost all such countries, Church and State are not fully separated.) The attitude that marriage continues "'til death do us part, no matter how miserable we may be" is also prevalent with certain groups in the United States. Thus, although this article focuses specifically on Argentina, it has much broader applicability.

On the day I was putting the final editorial touches on this article, the following appeared in *The Palm Beach Post* (Leigh, 1987):

LEGALIZING DIVORCE IN ARGENTINA FACES "STONE AGE" BARRIERS*

About two years ago, it occurred to former Judge Juan Baptista Sejean that under a strict interpretation of Argentine law, he and his second wife were crooks. Their offense: adultery.

Not that the two were cheating on each other. Argentina, along with the Philippines, Ireland, Paraguay, Malta and the European principalities of Andorra, . . . is one of the few countries in the world where divorce is illegal.

Under an 1888 Argentine statute, the separation of married couples is permitted but divorce and remarriage are not.

Source: Reprinted from "Legalizing Divorce in Argentina Faces 'Stone Age' Barriers" by C. Leigh, *The Palm Beach Post*, April 12, 1987, p.21A.

And Argentina, where a majority of the people are Catholic, is hosting a very prominent supporter of the status quo: Pope John Paul II.

The Pope's repeated denunciations of divorce as incompatible with the Christian concept of the family come at a sensitive time. In August, the country's chamber of deputies sanctioned a law permitting divorce and remarriage after couples had been separated for two years. The Argentine Senate almost certainly would have taken up the bill last year were it not for the announcement of the Pope's six-day visit.

Precedent Set

The former judge, who now has a private law practice, acted after reaching his intriguing conclusion about the legal status of himself and his second spouse. He demanded that Argentina's civil matrimony statute be declared unconstitutional and that his de facto divorce and second marriage both be legally recognized.

After losing the first two rounds, Sejean won in Argentina's Supreme Court in November. On March 30, he and his second wife, Alicia Natalia, who have been living together and considering themselves married since the time of Sejean's divorce, obtained their marriage license from the Civil Registry in Buenos Aires. It was an Argentine first (1987).

There's a big constituency for divorce in Argentina. There are an estimated 1 million couples in this nation of 30 million who would like to be considered man and wife under the law but aren't.

The lack of a divorce law "doesn't reflect Argentina's cultural reality," Sejean said. "But the influence of the Catholic Church is such that it has managed to cause more than 70 divorce bills to abort so far in this century."

Pope's Effect

There can be no "true love" if not "by way of a full commitment that lasts until death," the pontiff said.

"Only indissolvable matrimony will serve as a firm and lasting basis in the community of the family," he said.

Perhaps to avoid provoking criticism of Vatican interference in Argentine political affairs, the pontiff has rarely referred to divorce by name. But Argentina's bishops have not been as subtle.

After the chamber of deputies approved the divorce bill last year, in a 176–36 vote, the deputies who voted in favor began receiving letters from their local bishops urging them to repent publicly for the "sin committed" in the vote.

REFERENCES

Diaz Usandivaras, C., Filgueira de Casares, L., et al. (1986), *El impacto de la epistemologia sistemica en la asistencia legal y psicologica de la familia en proceso de divorcio*. Report submitted during the III Argentine Congress on Systemic Therapy, Buenos Aires.

Goldsmith, J. (1980). The postdivorce family system. In F. Walsh (Ed.), *Normal family processes*. New York: Guilford Press.

Haley, J. (1967). Towards a theory of pathological systems. In *Family therapy and disturbed families*. Palo Alto: Science and Behavior Books.

Haley, J. (1976). *Problem solving therapy*. San Francisco: Jossey Bass.

Haley, J. (1980). *Leaving home*. New York: McGraw Hill.

Kaslow, F. (1986). La mediacion en el divorcio. *Revista Terapia Familiar, 15*.

La Ley (1981). Civil Court, Room F, 116–803.

Leigh, C. (1987, April 12). Legalizing divorce in Argentina faces "Stone Age" barriers. *The Palm Beach Post*, p. 21a.

Madanes, C. (1981). *Strategic family therapy*. San Francisco: Jossey Bass.

Wagmaister, A., et al. (1986). Acuerdo entre conyuges en la proyectada reforma a la ley de matrimonio civil. *La Ley*.

Zavalia, R. (Ed.). (1986). *Codigo civil de la republica Argentina*. Buenos Aires:

3. Remarried Couples: The Architects of Stepfamilies

Florence W. Kaslow, PhD
Director
Florida Couples and Family Institute
and
Private Practice
West Palm Beach, Florida
and
Adjunct Professor of Medical Psychology
Department of Psychiatry
Duke University Medical Center
Durham, North Carolina

I s marriage "a community consisting of a master, a mistress, and two slaves—making in all two" as Bierce claimed in a *Devil's Dictionary* (1984)? Is it "the completest image of heaven and hell we are capable of receiving in this life" as Steele depicted it in *The Spectator* (1979)? Is it a series of painful compromises, an interminable conversation punctuated by disputes? Is it all of these and much, much more or less—depending on the two partners and the nature of their relationship and their personalities? Perhaps marriages are so varied, amorphous, and chameleon-like that they defy description as a single, or even multifaceted, phenomenon. Each one is unique, with some characteristics in common with other marriages and other characteristics that are idiosyncratic.

REMARRIAGE: A GROWING PHENOMENON

Although first marriages are hard to define and portray, remarriages and stepfamilies are even more complex. There is a vast array of possible pairings, such as

- both married before, but no children
- both married before, and each has children
- both married before, and only one has children
- one married before and has children, and one never married before

- one never married before, but has an out-of-wedlock child; and the other one never married before
- one never married before with no children, and one married before with no children

This list does not begin to take into account the unresolved and unfinished miscellaneous issues that may remain from the prior marriage, such as a painful experience of rejection and the financial entanglement with the former partner that continues until all child and spousal support payments end. Often, the new marriage must play host to a whole "cast of characters" who are perceived as ghosts from the past—ex-spouses, children who were not expected to "live-in" or visit often, former in-laws, old friends, and even bill collectors. Unless neither has children from the prior marriage, the couple does not have time alone together to establish themselves as a dyadic unit *before* they must deal with other members of the new family and all the preexisting bonds and conflicts that were created during the earlier marriage, the predivorce period, and the postdivorce single parenting phase (Bohannon, 1970; Kaslow, 1984). Thus, rarely is there sufficient time to build a solid foundation for the marriage before the couple must cope with the exigencies of step-parenting (Messinger, 1984; Visher & Visher, 1979), child and spousal support payments to be sent or that are not received on time, calls with complaints about visitation from an ex-spouse or requests (demands ?) for additional child support payments or to reduce existing ones, etc.

In light of all this, it seems amazing that 83% of divorced men and 75% of divorced women choose to remarry and that apparently 50% of these "make it" (i.e., remain married "'til death do us part") the second time around. Or, does it just seem that the odds are overwhelmingly stacked against the success of remarriage families because those on whom much of the literature is based (e.g., Goldner, 1982; Isaacs, 1982; Sager, Brown, Crohn, Engel, Rodstein & Walker, 1983); are distressed and caught in negative cycles of interaction that do not bode well for the future?

Namelessness: A Population Minus a Universally Accepted Label

In this article, a sample of the myriad problems which confront many, if not most, remarriage or REM families (the term utilized by Sager et al, 1983) will be illustrated through a case presentation and analysis. Various terms for families in which one or both spouses have been married before, such as *blended, reconstituted, recoupled, REM*, and *stepfamily*, are used interchangeably in the field. None seems to capture the essence of these families adequately, however. For example, remarried, reconstituted, and recoupled all seem to imply that the original couple have reunited. Blended connotes a merging together, as if the separate identities of the parts are obliterated. Yet, it is important that the children in the new family retain an awareness of and a close relationship with both of their biological parents (Boszormenyi-Nagy & Spark, 1973; Sager et al., 1983) and that their identification with the nonresidential parent not be lost in a blending (Ahrons & Rodgers, 1987; Kaslow & Schwartz, 1987; Saposnek, 1983; Wallerstein & Kelly, 1980).

Perception of the Step-Parent

The word *stepfamily*, particularly as it subsumes the word *stepmother*, conjures up for many the vision of the wicked stepmother so indelibly etched in their memory in childhood when they first heard the stories of Snow White, Cinderella, Hansel and Gretel, and many other disconcerting tales. Unfortunately, the persistence of the myth of the wicked stepmother seems to set the stage for a self-fulfilling prophecy in that children may expect their father's new wife to be mean, inconsiderate, demanding, and rude. If their mother or others accuse her of any or all of the above and/or they know or suspect that she was involved with their father before their parents' separation or divorce, the children may project the blame onto their stepmother for alienating their father's affection and causing their parents' marriage to fail. It is, of course, more ego-syntonic for children to blame a heretofore outsider than to see their father's responsibility for his choices and behavior. In turn, the stepmother may well resent her husband's accusatory, nonwelcoming, and "bratty" children. Should her husband be unwilling to set limits for his children and to uphold her right to do so, her resentment increases. In order to avoid being taken advantage of as their maid, the stepmother may become shrewish and demanding—fulfilling the children's fears and expectations.

How revealing it is that literature for young children does not seem to have a male counterpart in the form of a wicked stepfather. Perhaps the closest character is Fagin in Dickens' *Oliver Twist* (1984), and he is more an antisocial, exploitative, yet slightly devoted foster father to a group of street urchins than a stepfather in the traditional sense. Furthermore, young people are not introduced to Dickens until many years after they have left the nursery so that they are not as impressionable when they first encounter Fagin. Future stepfathers are more commonly described by society and by many temporarily single mothers as a "rescuer" who will help take care of the family financially and emotionally. Thus, many stepfathers enter the family scene on a more neutral, even positive, basis than do stepmothers. Hopefully, a better, more benign term than any of those alluded to above will emerge to encompass this growing portion of families in our society.

It is hoped that the following case description, analysis, and discussion of the intervention process will illuminate some of the typical dilemmas that confront remarriage families. Not every issue confronted by REM families was exhibited in the family under consideration nor, of course, do all reconstituted families have all or most of these problems. This represents an illustration of a remarriage family that is in a way a composite of many we have treated at the Florida Couples and Family Institute from 1981–1987.

CASE EXAMPLE

The Roaring Family*

Jerry R. requested therapy for himself and Sherry, his wife of 3 months. He was already concerned that his choice of a second wife had been a big mistake and wanted help in deciding whether to try to improve this young and troubled marriage or to dissolve it quickly, "cutting" his and his children's losses and disappointments.

At the intake interview, Jerry, a 39-year-old almost senior level executive in a mid-sized corporation, was neat, well-groomed, attractive, and highly controlled. His voice was well modulated; he seemed quite rational, articulate, and "nice." By contrast, Sherry, a 34-year-old assistant to a junior level manager in the same corporation, was slightly disheveled, somewhat histrionic, tense, and anxious. They appeared to be an "odd couple." Jerry had a master's degree in business administration from a prestigious university. Sherry had a high school diploma equivalent. He seemed to be upper middle class and upwardly mobile; she appeared to be lower middle class and not at all ambitious. Her personality seemed to be dependent and hostile; daily coping, even just surviving, was absorbing all of her energies.

Jerry and Sherry had met at work and found each other quite attractive. Sherry was already divorced and had custody of her 12-year-old daughter, Kim. After her divorce, she and Kim had moved into her parents' home—which she had eagerly left 16 years earlier because she could "not stand" her parents and brothers. Both parents had been and still were alcoholics. Uneducated, downtrodden, they lived a hand-to-mouth existence. Sherry had

---

*Certain data have been changed sufficiently to disguise and protect the identity of the family involved.

left home through the only route acceptable to her parents—
"marriage to the first guy who asked me." She had been physically abused by Guy, her first husband, and had recklessly sought
solace through drugs and alcohol. Guy also became involved in
drugs and became a dealer to support their habit. Three years
before she entered therapy, after a series of episodes in which
Guy abused her and Kim, Sherry had been able to mobilize enough
energy to overcome the protestations of her family and his, and
get a divorce. Several months later, Guy was killed in a drug-
related shootout. Both families held her accountable, saying that
he had taken up dangerous activities because she had abandoned
him. She carried a huge burden of guilt and confusion about her
ex-husband's death and had never fully discussed it with Kim.

Living with her parents was devastating for Sherry. She found
their alcoholism and bickering disgusting and their home a nox-
ious environment in which to raise Kim. When she began to date
Jerry and told him about her desperate desire, really need, to
leave her parents, Jerry felt sorry for her. Because she could not
afford a place of her own, he invited her to move in with him for a
while and bring her daughter along. Eagerly and gratefully, she
accepted.

Jerry had been divorced approximately 15 months earlier. He
had primary custody of his 12-year-old daughter, Karen, and his
16-year-old son, Tom. An extremely devoted father, he was
delighted to have his children with him. He and the children had
become a close and interdependent threesome in the period
following his divorce. The children resented the intrusive entry of
Sherry and Kim into their home. By the time that the family sought
therapy a year later, the mutual hostility had not abated; if anything, it had intensified.

Sherry's use of alcohol and drugs had progressed into obvious
and serious substance abuse after she moved in with Jerry. The
children often saw her stoned or inebriated. She was slovenly and
did few of the homemaking tasks. Jerry's ex-wife, Lana, petitioned for custody of the children because she did not want her
children to be with "that drunken whore." Jerry, a compassionate
rescuer who had been smitten by Sherry's dependence and
wanton charm, had been unable to ask her to leave. His ex-wife
regained custody of the children—a loss that he deeply resented
and for which he secretly blamed Sherry. He insisted that she go
into a residential drug and alcohol detoxification program, which
she did for a month. During that time, Jerry cared for Kim and saw

his own children often. Kim and Karen formed a good relationship and began to regard each other as sisters. This was one of the few positives to accrue from the new pseudo-family.

When Sherry left the treatment program, the staff felt that her prognosis was guarded. They considered her an addictive, dependent personality—fragile, volatile, and likely to resort to substance abuse again when "the going got rough." Her attendance at Narcotics Anonymous (NA) and Alcoholics Anonymous (AA) meetings was irregular. Nonetheless, she felt that she wanted to "clean up my act and live respectably" and convinced Jerry, who apparently did not need much urging, to marry her. Appalled and angry, his children felt cast off by him and replaced by Sherry. Because Jerry was lenient with them, partially because it appeased his guilt and partially because he was by nature "laid back" about scheduling, they rarely adhered to the set visitation times. Both of his children had rooms at his home—Tom, his own room, and Karen, a room that she shared with Kim—and they came and went whenever they felt so inclined. Sherry needed the structure of a schedule to feel any degree of comfort, however; predictability made her feel safer, and flexibility produced chaos.

The disagreements about Jerry's children had led to escalating marital conflict, and it was at this point that Jerry called to enter therapy. The therapist's initial impression was that Sherry desperately wanted the marriage to continue, but was floundering. She was still a month shy of a year of sobriety and was determined not to slip back into addiction. Her success to date provided the therapist with an area in which to affirm her strength and her ability to grow and change. Yet, as a result of the glaring deficits in her background, she was an ungratified oral-dependent personality. Her neediness was so acute that she felt she had to compete with Jerry's children, as well as with Kim, for Jerry's love and attention. When she did not get her way, she erupted with explosive rage and alienated everyone further. Jerry was embarrassed and infuriated by her "selfish outbursts." The more he gave, the more she seemed to demand. Like many spouses of a "borderline personality" (APA, 1980), he indicated that he "never could seem to give enough." He said that he could no longer tolerate her jealous rages when he wanted to spend time alone with his son fishing or playing tennis on the weekend. Conversely, she felt that he sabotaged her recovery by wanting her to make and serve special dinners on the nights that his children visited them—even if this interfered with her attendance at an NA or AA meeting. He rarely attended AL Anon sessions, claiming that the addiction was her problem, not his.

Jerry periodically became incensed that Sherry felt free to spend part of her salary and an insurance reserve fund left to Kim by her father on clothing and outings for her daughter without checking with him regarding the state of their overall family budget. Yet, whenever he wanted to supplement the child support he sent his ex-wife by buying his children clothing or other gifts, or by giving them additional allowance, Sherry screamed at his overindulgence and expenditure of their money on "pampering" his children. Her rationalization was that he already sent child support and that his children had a second parent plus two sets of generous grandparents to provide for them, while she was Kim's only source of support.

THEMES AND PROBLEMS IN THE REMARRIED FAMILY

It was quite evident that the three children had been very intertwined in their parents' lives before the inception of the relationship between Jerry and Sherry. The adults' special attachments to their respective children following the dissolution of each of their marriages were strong and seemingly predictable. As the live-in relationship became a fait accompli, these bonds were threatened by the intensity and excitement of the new love affair. In reality, the intimacy of the one-on-one adult psychosexual pairing pushed the parent-child ties from first place in the emotional lives of the two adults, creating resentment in the children, who once again felt displaced and insecure. It was not surprising that Jerry's children, who lost their beloved and attentive father as primary residential parent, blamed their intrusive stepmother. Her entry into their home had triggered their departure and significant losses. Conversely, Sherry's daughter gained an attractive and nurturing father, a more solid home base, and a much wanted sister.

Ghosts from the Past and Not So Hidden Rivalries

Unresolved issues from prior marriages often haunt the remarriage family.

In the R. family, Lana, the first Mrs. R., not only petitioned successfully to regain primary physical custody of Tom and Karen, but also continued to call her ex-husband to reemphasize the children's complaints about Sherry and to denigrate Sherry as a person. Not wanting to antagonize Lana further and thereby risk additional alienation of his children, Jerry tolerated her criticisms passively and permitted her and the children total flexibility regarding visitation. Both of these attitudes infuriated Sherry and threw all her attempts to bring order into her chaotic life into continuous upheaval.

Similarly, Sherry was plagued by guilt and worry about having divorced, thereby abandoning her ex-husband, and perhaps having inadvertently contributed to his death. Her own family of origin demeaned her through such accusations. Any contact with them stirred her up for days. Furthermore, because of her inability to really discuss Kim's father's death with the child, Kim remained confused and uneasy. The former partners' lingering impact contributed to the ongoing tensions and strained competition between Lana, who had not remarried, and Sherry. Often, ex-husbands remarry before their ex-wives do, and an interactive pattern similar to that which prevailed in their first marriage evolves.

Money: The Unfinished Economic Connection

It is rare for the economic marriage to end simultaneously with the legal marriage (Bohannon, 1970; Kaslow & Schwartz, 1987). This is apt to occur only when the marriage has been short-lived, there are no children, and any financial settlement is to be paid off at the time of the issuance of the divorce decree or shortly thereafter. In the overwhelming majority of cases, there are children, and child support payments must continue as part of postdivorce parenting at least until the youngest child is 18 years of age and frequently until that child completes college. In this sense, many divorced couples want to continue to provide for their children in appropriate ways into young adulthood, just as do their still married counterparts.

It is not uncommon for a second wife to feel resentful or deprived of what she wants (and may have been led to believe she would get) for the new family when her husband sends money to his ex-wife for their children, particularly if there is not enough money to go around easily. Given the fact that money is usually sent weekly, bimonthly, or monthly, the annoyance is often recurrent. A battle may be waged each time the husband sends money to the ex-spouse or children and each time they overtly ask or subtly convey the need for more.

All these factors existed in the R. family. In addition, by the time the family entered therapy, Jerry had volunteered to pay for Tom's tuition and books at a local college. Tom was not a particularly good student, and Sherry sincerely believed that "Jerry is wasting our money on his dumb, unambitious son." She felt that, if Tom wanted to go to college, he should pay his own way. Since she did not anticipate that Kim might want to go to college, she was not confronted with a future inequity of expecting Jerry to help pay for her daughter's education but not his son's. And college did not rank as a high priority in Sherry's life schema.

In many instances, the judge who issues the divorce decree orders the husband to send predetermined spousal support payments to his ex-wife for many years to come. This continuing economic encumbrance infuriates many second wives; they are unable to comprehend: (1) Why should he keep supporting her when he gets absolutely nothing in return except aggravation? (and, of course, she doesn't want him to get anything positive in return). (2) Is it fair that she can afford to stay home and not work because of the child plus spousal support he sends her, and I have to work so that we can make ends meet? (3) How can he say no to me when I or my child want or need something, when he either complies with her demands willingly or she can take him to court and have the judge insist that he provide whatever she says her children must have (e.g., camp, orthodontia)? This scenario does not set the stage for harmonious interplay in many stepfamilies.

In the R. family, Sherry worked out of financial necessity, not because of a desire to achieve in or express herself through a career. Her hatred of the idle and well-supported former Mrs. R. bubbled out like exploding lava.

Noxious Behaviors

Individuals bring everything that they have become into a new marriage. Some couples resolve not to allow petty things to bother them, as they do not wish to hurt each other's feelings or their relationship by being critical or picayune. Often, trivial annoyances were a major source of distress in the earlier marriage, so the individuals resolve to be tolerant in the new marriage. Over time, however, these annoyances begin to seem less trivial, particularly when time alone together is a rarity and so many problems center around the children.

Sherry disliked Tom's messiness and "hanging out" alone in his room, silent behind closed doors. She also railed against his freedom to come and go without a schedule. She abhorred Karen's confrontative outspokenness; "sassy" disobedience violated her code of acceptable behavior from "punk kids." Jerry's passive acquiescence to the demands of his ex-wife and his children, coupled with his critical attacks on her earlier addictive behavior, his current failure to nurture his children, and his inflexibility concerning household tasks, were chronic sources of irritation to her. Jerry held her substance abuse and need to "do an AA program" in disdain. The threads holding their fledgling remarriage together were indeed precariously strung.

Sexual Attraction: Incest in the Stepfamily

The taboos against brother-sister or father-daughter sexual relationships are not as clear or strong in remarriage families as they are in nuclear families (Phipps, 1986). A stepsister and stepbrother may well be sexually attracted to one another, particularly in the atmosphere of heightened sexuality that is often pervasive in the early months of a marriage. Unwittingly and unsuspectingly, the new parent couple often foster this attraction by expressing great pleasure and relief in how well their two adolescents get along and encouraging them to do things together. Similarly, the wife may be delighted that her new husband likes her daughter and is willing to help her do difficult homework, learn to drive a car, or complete other projects. She may bask in the obvious affection that they have for each other, never thinking that it has become sexualized and her "little girl" is now her rival for her husband's sexual—not parental—attentions.

Other Themes

Other prevalent themes revolve around inlaws, where children are to spend holidays, whether to retain former possessions or start afresh, and whose apartment or house to live in or whether the new couple should immediately establish a residence for their current marriage and family. As to the last, it is this author's opinion that a new territory that belongs to this union is highly preferable.

THE COURSE OF TREATMENT

Phase I

The initial phase of treatment with Jerry and Sherry consisted of history taking and the construction of a joint genogram in my office, during which they spontaneously talked about the people in their complex family tree and their feelings toward these people (Kaslow, 1984; McGoldrick & Gerson, 1985). This dynamic family map provided a graphic depiction of who "belonged to" and related to whom. Many ambivalent feelings and memories were evoked in this process, and some catharsis occurred.

Because they had never discussed their expectations of each other and of the relationship prior to deciding to marry, three sessions were spent on having them articulate (1) what they wanted and needed, (2) what they were willing to give to each other, and (3) what expectations they did not think they could fulfill. This contracting process (Sager et al., 1983) helped them clarify why they had been attracted to each other, what needs were and were not being met, and where they were *at this point in time*. Bringing their focus into the present dislodged them from the positions in which they were mired—he still harping on his disgust with her addiction and rudeness to his children, she decrying his preference for spending time with his children rather than with her and his benign neglect of her wishes.

Sherry decided to go to a minimum of one AA meeting a week, to two whenever possible. Jerry agreed to go to Al Anon at least once a month. They agreed that she had done well in maintaining her sobriety and that this had to remain a major goal. Jerry's long overdue acknowledgment of her efforts to overcome her addiction was valuable to her. The therapist was able to convey to him the importance of his accepting that Sherry had progressed from her "drunken whore" stage and was living a quite sober and respectable life. Furthermore, wasn't it high time that his children recognized this and stopped treating her like a despicable character? In grateful response, Sherry was able to cease nagging Tom about his room and to become more flexible about the visitation schedule. Jerry and Sherry began setting aside at least one night per weekend to go out as an adult couple, either alone or with friends, and Sherry made a valiant and partially successful effort to control her impulsivity and temper.

Phase II

Once a better equilibrium had been established, a long session was held with Sherry, Jerry, and the three children. To everyone's surprise, Sherry was able to listen, absorb what was said, and not react defensively. Kim, who looked young for her age, was giggly and somewhat sheepish. She barely spoke and seemed to have copied her mother's pattern of not talking about emotion-laden issues. Karen's disappointment in her father and her anger with and dislike of Sherry were quickly disclosed in her responses to queries about what it was like for her when Sherry and Kim moved in, when her mother regained custody of her and Tom, when Sherry went for detoxification, when her father and Sherry decided to marry, and now. Through her sadness, hurt, sense of loss, and confusion at her father's choice, an intelligent, sensitive, and forthright adolescent emerged. After the therapist commented on Karen's courage in being honest and candid, Tom, who had been quite tentative and detached, expressed a growing liking for Sherry; a willingness to cooperate at their home now that their expectations had been clarified; and a great deal of concern about his educational and vocational options, as well as the extent of emotional and financial support that he could expect. His father indicated that Tom would have exactly the same support that he would have had if the original marriage had not collapsed. Sherry winced at the idea of any additional financial commitment to his son, Tom, especially if it entailed increased tuition, room, and board at a college away from home. This issue needs continued work in treatment with this couple, just as the economic issues do for many remarried families who are experiencing extreme turbulence.

Karen and Tom raised another issue, one about which Jerry had indicated concern in previous sessions. They wanted to spend time alone with their father on weekend visits. They were peeved at Sherry's resistance to and resentment of this idea. With the therapist, the family explored the validity of this desire and the importance of the biological ties within the context of the remarriage family system. The therapist listened empathically to Sherry's fear that they would form an alliance so tight that it would exclude her and Kim. She disclosed her fears about losing Jerry to his children.

At the behavioral level, it was agreed in this session that Jerry might spend time alone with Tom and Karen, separately or together, part of each Saturday that they visit. Friday evening was to be family night, and Saturday night was to be the night that Jerry and his wife go out as a couple. Sherry remains uneasy with this plan, which is just being put into operation. The thought of sharing Jerry activates her deep-seated sense of deprivation and her hunger for more nurturance gets activated at the thought of sharing Jerry. As in most remarried families, the couple must

balance their commitment to their own children with the commitment to their new mate. The therapist is continuing to focus
attention on the many ways that Sherry can attempt to fill the void
deep within, such as attending AA meetings; forming a close
relationship with a sponsor (not yet done); doing things with Kim
while Jerry is busy with Karen and Tom, something she has never
done; spending time with women friends; and having Jerry
devote some blocks of time and energy exclusively to her
throughout each week.

Whereas ordinarily the therapist might do family-of-origin sessions separately with the spouses and their respective parents
and siblings (Framo, 1981), this seems contraindicated in this
case. This couple agreed that Sherry's attempts to do repair work
with her parents and become a respected adult in the family
(Williamson, 1981) have resulted only in their ridicule of her for
becoming a "goodie-goodie," "being on the wagon," and being
too "uptown" for their family.

Therapeutic work is in progress on the themes of Jerry's passive controlling maneuvers, his excessive leniency with his children, and his very tentative commitment to his relationship with
Sherry in terms of closeness and intimacy. Whereas some people
enter a remarriage with the intention of doing everything possible
to make the marriage work, Jerry belongs to the group who think
in terms of "if I don't like it, I can leave—as I did before" and "the
second divorce is bound to be easier than the first."

The therapist's role has combined sympathetic listening, circular questioning, clarification and interpretation, confrontation,
provocative and paradoxical comments, behavioral suggestions,
restructuring, and ego support. Although the primary modality has
been couples therapy from a family systems perspective, treatment has included an individual session with each spouse and
one family session. The future pattern is to be three couple
sessions to continue to strengthen the unity of the spousal dyad,
followed by one family session to provide an opportunity for the
full remarriage family to resolve prickly issues and bond more
closely into a compatible unit. This approach flows from the
"diaclectic" (Kaslow, 1981) or integrative model.

In treatment with most remarriage families, it is necessary to dispel not only
the myth of the wicked stepmother, a role into which Sherry had most
definitely been cast, but also the myth of instant love, affection, and respect
between members of the newly created family (Einstein, 1982). Such attach-

ments evolve only with time, a sense of humor, and good will. Any unresolved grief work regarding the demise of the previous marriage must be completed before sufficient psychic energy and trust are available to invest in a remarriage. Power issues often surface, and they must be negotiated so that the couple/family develops effective problem-solving techniques for those future occasions when battles for control erupt. Only then can conflict-ridden remarriage families have a good prognosis for their third chance families to co-evolve well and to live reasonably satisfying lives together. Family conferences for planning and for problem resolution should ultimately supplant therapy sessions.

CONCLUSION

In treating remarriage families, it is important to remember that people enter second or third marriages with high hopes and much caution. They bring along unfulfilled dreams from the past and much excess baggage. The therapist who works with remarriage families must be able to differentiate the clinical issues (e.g., personality dysfunction like Sherry's addictive behavior and extreme dependency) from the step-family issues (e.g., the children's inability to accept a parent's new partner and love interest). Therapists who are not conversant with the existential realities of the formation of a remarried family may find themselves searching for clinical pathology which can explain the difficulty. In reality, however, the ways in which remarriage families respond to the special dilemmas created by their structure are often predicated on intrapsychic distress and general difficulties with close interpersonal relationships. All these become intertwined issues, compelling attention in therapy.

In addition, clinical issues can heighten the marital schism and make the process of building a joint, new terrain more difficult. For example, when a step-parent who as a child was embedded in a family triangle marries a biological parent who was a family rebel, they are likely to re-experience their insider-outsider dilemmas. It is incumbent on family therapists to enable remarriage couples to understand the ways in which the stepfamily structure contributes to a high level of discomfort and tension for all. With everyone's cooperation, patience, acceptance, and ability to perceive and enjoy the absurdity inherent in this family form, the remarriage family can flourish as a viable entity—especially if the individual members also accept responsibility for their own growth.

REFERENCES

Ahrons, C.R., & Rodgers, R.H. (1987). *Divorced families: A multidisciplinary developmental view.* New York: W.W. Norton.

American Psychiatric Association. (1980). *Diagnostic and statistical manual: III.* Washington, DC: Author.

Bierce, A. (1984). *Devil's dictionary.* Mattituck, NY: Ameron. (Revision of 1911 edition)

Bohannan, P. (1970). The six stations of divorce. In P. Bohannan (Ed.), *Divorce and after: An analysis of the emotional and social problems of divorce* (pp. 29–55). New York: Doubleday.

Boszormenyi-Nagy, I., & Spark, G. (1973). *Invisible loyalties.* New York: Harper & Row.

Dickens, C. (1984). *Oliver Twist.* New York: Dodd Mead.

Einstein, E. (1982). *The stepfamily: Living, loving and learning.* New York: Macmillan.

Framo, J. (1981). The integration of marital therapy with sessions with the family of origin. In A.S. Gurman & D.P. Kniskern (Eds.), *Handbook of family therapy.* (pp. 133–158). New York: Brunner/Mazel.

Goldner, V. (1982). Therapeutic techniques for remarriage families. In J. Hansen & L. Messinger (Eds.), *Therapy with remarriage families* (pp. 195–206). Rockville, MD: Aspen Publishers.

Isaacs, M.B. (1982). Helping Mom fail: A case of a stalemated divorcing process. *Family Process.* *21,*(2), 225–234.

Kaslow, F.W. (1981). A diaclectic approach to family therapy and practice: Selectivity and synthesis. *Journal of Marital and Family Therapy, 7,*(3), 345–351.

Kaslow, F.W. (1984). Divorce: An evolutionary process of change in the family system. *Journal of Divorce, 7,*(3), 21–39.

Kaslow, F.W. (1986). An intensive training experience: A six day post graduate institute model. *Journal of Psychotherapy and the Family, 1,*(4), 73–82.

Kaslow, F.W., & Schwartz, L.L. (1987). *Dynamics of divorce: A life cycle perspective.* New York: Brunner/Mazel.

McGoldrick, M., & Gerson, R. (1985). *Genograms in family assessment.* New York: Norton.

Messinger, L. (1984). *Remarriage: A family affair.* New York: Plenum.

Phipps, E. (1986). Sexual tensions in a remarried family. *Contemporary Family Therapy, 8,*(3), 208–216.

Sager, C.J., Brown, H.S., Crohn, H., Engel, T., Rodstein, E., & Walker, L. (1983). *Treating the remarried family.* New York: Brunner/Mazel.

Saposnek, D.T. (1983). *Mediating child custody disputes.* San Francisco: Jossey-Bass.

Steele, R., & Addison, J. (1979). *The spectator.* Tottowa, NJ: Littlefield Adams. (Reproduction of 1945 edition)

Visher, E.B., & Visher, J.S. (1979). *Stepfamilies: A guide to working with stepparents and step-children.* New York: Brunner/Mazel.

Wallerstein, J.S., & Kelly, J.B. (1980). *Surviving the breakup: How children and parents cope with divorce.* New York: Basic Books.

Williamson, D.S. (1981). Personal authority via termination of the intergenerational hierarchical boundary: A 'new' stage in the family life cycle. *Journal of Marital and Family Therapy, 7,*(4), 441–452.

Part II
Treating Couples Who Manifest Specific Disorders or Syndromes

4. Couples in the Creative Arts

Joan C. Barth, PhD
Family Therapist
Doylestown, Pennsylvania
and
Former Counseling Psychologist
The Curtis Institute of Music
Philadelphia, Pennsylvania

I n his groundbreaking work, *The Artist in Society,* Hatterer (1965) stated that the "sources of creativity and explanations of the artist's personality are more complex than any of the present, overworked psychiatric theories" (p. 20). More than 20 years later, little has been added to his theories, and there is no major theory about the particular problems that arise in the marriages of individuals who are both in the arts. Those in the arts have significant differences from individuals of the same age in other fields, however, particularly in their notions of time, space, authority, and methods of problem solving.

THE PROFESSIONAL IN THE CREATIVE ARTS

The definition of a professional as a person who receives pay for full-time work in a specialized occupation does not apply to persons in the creative arts. A study of writers who had been featured on the front page of *The New York Times Book Review* recently revealed that none of them earned more than $10,000 a year from their writing (Rooney, 1985). They all supplemented their income by working in other fields. Despite the fact that some actors derive most of their income from waiting tables, that some writers pay their mortgages by teaching English, and that some artists do paste-up for newspapers, they all define themselves respectively as actors, writers, and artists— not waiters, teachers, or paste-up clerks.

The creative arts may be defined as the development of nonessential products that can be exhibited and priced; therefore, a person in the creative arts is one who conceives of and may develop such products. This definition makes no distinction between those in the fine arts and those in the applied or performing arts. A man who draws quick sketches on the plaza in Santa Fe and a woman whose oil paintings hang in the National Gallery of Art may both refer to themselves as artists. Their self-labels are the ones that a therapist must accept.

Because an artist does not always accept the reality agreed on by the majority, a rigid therapeutic definition of the professional in the creative arts is inconsistent with the artist's very core mentality—his or her responsibility to define the world through personal vision. Things as they exist are not as real to an artist as are things as they might be. Unlike psychotics, however, artists can clearly differentiate between their own creative productions and the reality perceived by the masses.

Some therapists have been trained to provide speedy, concise diagnoses on the basis of the *Diagnostic and Statistical Manual* (APA, 1980). In contrast, the artist's training encourages postponement of judgment on an idea and the exploration of various ways to attack a problem. Therefore, therapy for couples in the arts must support their own style of problem consideration. It may be futile, for example, to adhere to a preformed notion of appropriate therapy with couples in the arts. Rather, a clinician must recognize the likelihood that such a couple has already attempted traditional solutions. It is not unusual for them to have studied numerous books and articles on the area of conflict, just as if they were composing a new score or constructing a scale model of a building in order to analyze the light from all sides.

> A musician in a major symphony orchestra and his artist wife described one unsuccessful course of treatment with a psychiatrist: "He was a real nice man and we liked him, but he didn't help us much." The psychiatrist "was a bit of a musician himself" and liked talking music with the husband. The wife received individual help in learning relaxation techniques. The therapist's usefulness to them as a couple was in giving them an opportunity to discuss the problems created by the husband's schizophrenic daughter from a former marriage. He carried out the role of "Dr. Homeostat," a therapist who allows clients to stay in balance, but not to expand (Bergman, 1985).

DEVELOPMENT OF AN ARTIST'S MENTALITY

Many musicians, writers, painters, architects, and others in the arts cannot remember a time when they were not interested in their fields. "I imitated my

15-year-old sister's piano pieces by heart when I was 3," said a pianist from California. A painter in Massachusetts said that his first memory was of a "gridwork on my bedroom floor. I was about 1½." Such artists cannot keep from being absorbed in their work. Some of their families encourage their artistic development; others do not.

In families that accept the arts as a life option, it is easy to pursue the development of a talent. Some families place deterrents in the artist's path, however, making such statements as "all dancers are faggots" or "you'll never find a husband in that bunch of weirdos." Parents of daughters in the arts seem less concerned about the possibility of making a living through artistic pursuits than do parents of sons. Expectations fall along obvious stereotypical lines. A daughter can marry a man who will "take care of her"; a son cannot, unless he marries a wealthy woman.

In formal training, artists may become overly dependent on teachers for reassurance, encouragement, and advice, especially when they do not receive support from home. This dependence may become an impediment to the students' personal growth, causing them to be overly vulnerable to flattery and to allow others to determine if their work is good. They may become victims of another person's dreams.

> A singing teacher was enraged with one of her students for singing at a city market for money. At the time, he had a quarter in his pocket and nothing to eat in his cupboard. His teacher's dream was for him to sing in the Metropolitan Opera House. She saw him only as a possible fulfillment of her dream, not as a person.

People in the arts must learn to deal with situations that young people in most other fields are spared. Frequent rejection notices, audition failures, and negative criticisms of their work are everyday occurrences. When their work has received cruel reviews, they frequently pursue their work more determinedly than before. *Artists must grasp the fact that rejection is simply the opinion of another, not the final word on their work.* Their ego either becomes stronger or collapses under such criticism.

Unlike those in other fields, who may end work at 5:00 PM, creative artists work all the time. One musician stopped his therapy session when he heard the insistent sound of an E tone produced by the horn of a taxi caught in traffic. He was unable to limit his musical attention to the hours of class and practice. He lived it. McMullan (1976) called this quality of being focused on artistic goals while maintaining a "relaxed attention" that allows the artist always to keep a door open to learning a "flexible persistence." As Rogers (1961) said, "The complete openness of awareness to what exists at this moment is, I believe, an important condition of constructive creativity" (p. 354). To be so absorbed can be very satisfying. Rather than being bored by their work, artists are often impatient to return to it from other pursuits. William Styron said, "writing is hell," and "I'm simply the happiest, the placidest, when I'm writing" (Rose, 1981). It is not uncommon for artists to write, paint, or compose into the early morning hours—and to enjoy such work.

The ability to spend long periods of time alone doing one's work is essential to the artist. Enjoying one's own company is one of the necessities, as well as one of the pleasures, of an artist's development. Self-designed ideas are exciting companions. Characters, for example, develop a real dimension and provide company during the long solitary hours that the writer needs to produce a novel.

There is an exuberance about one's art that is like a long draught of an elixir of life. Feelings can seem abnormal, however, because few others articulate them in the same way. When an artist discovers that others share similar and even more colorful experiences, it is reassuring. In fact, it has been suggested that some artists (notably, the poet Emily Dickinson) have developed less than expected because they were deprived of the company and feedback of their colleagues.

RELATIONSHIP ISSUES

While many teen-agers concentrate on establishing dating relationships, young artists continue to develop their work during those years. Their apparent ease with adults who are fellow professionals often makes teen-agers in the arts seem more self-confident than they actually are. They may be comfortable discussing Bach with an adult, but not discussing the newest lipstick color with another teen-ager.

Teen-agers in the arts understand why classmates with similar interests may become socially unavailable for weeks as work on a specific artistic project totally absorbs them, even though other school friends may view these unavailable artists as unfriendly. Some young artists may find less satisfaction in socializing than in completing a manuscript, learning a new piece of music, or painting a canvas. They may prefer to find fun and intimate experiences in attending a play rehearsal or a concert, sketching marathon runners, or erecting a model of a building with like-minded souls.

Rogers (1961) described what he called "the anxiety of separateness" by imagining the creative person saying "I am alone. No one has ever done just this before. I have ventured into territory where no one has been. Perhaps I am foolish, or wrong, or lost, or abnormal." According to Rogers, these feelings evoke in the artist a desire to communicate as a way to "assuage the anxiety of separateness and assure himself that he belongs to the group" (p. 356).

Marriage

- "I wasn't ready for marriage when I got married. I was 21. But I knew she was for me. When I would be ready who knew where she'd be?" So stated a furniture designer about his artist wife.
- A composer explained that he wanted to marry because being an artist often meant loneliness, and he wanted someone who would be devoted to him. He loves being married to an artist; "she always encourages me." (One cannot help but wonder, of course, what direction her own artistic development will take as a result of her dedication to him.)

Other artists long for a family and marry to have children. Their families of origin sometimes continue financial support (e.g., paying for the grand-children to attend private schools). Parents of artists often seem willing to underwrite the work of their children. If so, they seldom badger their artistic offspring, nor do they openly lament the fact that their offspring are earning only a small income.

Marriage to someone in the same subspecialty of the arts seems most likely to present problems:

- One opera singer who was on tour for months at a time wanted to be married because it provided him with a sense of roots. After three marriages to women in opera, he married a secretary who was interested in opera merely as a spectator. She devoted herself to him with no attempt to develop a professional career of her own.
- One couple were both flutists. The husband was exceptionally talented, while the wife was only adequately so. They competed for the same jobs, and the husband usually won them. Professional competition eventually created insurmountable problems in the marriage, and they divorced.

Although a marriage between two artists with dissimilar talents—a writer and a musician, for example—entails less competition, the artistic pressures are similar. Thus, the spouses are likely to understand and empathize with one another.

In the practical realm (e.g., preparing dinner, doing laundry, going to the post office or drycleaners), couples state that they share equal responsibility. "Whoever sees that something needs to be done, does it." In reality, however, roles are gender-related. Wives are more likely to go to the grocery store, tend to the household chores, shop for the children's sneakers, make social commit-ments, and maintain contact with relatives. On the other hand, husbands are more likely to take responsibility for car and plumbing repairs.

The practical importance of the work involved in taking care of a home and family often receives little acknowledgment from either spouse. Such activities are perceived as merely necessary, mundane, and uninteresting. This may be one reason that artistic women in long-term marriages become depressed. They receive no acknowledgment for either their art or their homemaking talents.

Reasons for Seeking Marital Therapy

Like most married couples, couples who work in the creative arts do not seek help as soon as problems arise. In fact, one of their strengths is that they are accustomed to creating strategies for working out their own problems. Their training has prepared them to seek expert advice when their own resources have been depleted, however:

- A writer addicted to alcohol, particularly when his work was not progressing as he liked, was urged by his wife, a musician, to see a counselor with her. Only because his alcohol problem was hampering his work was he willing to seek treatment. It was not because his problem was affecting his wife.
- An actress and her painter husband sought therapy because she was fearful that her husband's depression about his lack of success in his profession made it necessary that she not succeed in hers. Despite the fact that she had received numerous offers for roles, she refused them on the ground that she might overshadow him and, thus, increase his depression.

Because so many artists have sought professional help for personal problems at some time in their lives, the use of therapy to achieve personal and professional growth does not appear abnormal. Many artists view family therapy as a kind of generous act. Because it usually does not identify a villain, it is more easily accepted than marital therapy, which magnifies the sense of blame and fault.

CASE STUDIES: DYNAMICS AND TREATMENT

Gunnar and Emily

Gunnar came from a family dominated by a very successful father, the editor of a national magazine. His three sisters had each married a man very strong in his field—one in chemistry, another in financial planning, and the third in industry. Of the four children, Gunnar was the only one competing with his father in the arts. Although he was an excellent writer like his father, he chose to concentrate on painting. Within that field, he restricted himself to the expression of pain and suffering—children dying of malnutrition, emaciated Holocaust survivors, and parents mourning a child's death.

Emily was a beautiful woman who had performed in a number of small acting roles off-Broadway. She came from a wealthy Southern family in which being an actress was considered a daring career choice. She had a younger sister who followed the more traditional path of marriage to an attorney in Richmond. About the time that Emily was being offered larger roles by better known directors, she met Gunnar and, after a whirlwind courtship, married him. They had three children in quick succession, and Emily settled down to life as a housewife in a Westchester community. With substantial monetary support from their families of origin, Gunnar and Emily lived a comfortable life.

At the point when their two older children left home for college, Gunnar and Emily experienced a marital crisis. Someone told them that Gunnar was undergoing a male mid-life crisis and should have an affair. He subsequently did become infatuated with an artist, but pulled back from a sexual relationship with her.

The other woman flattered Gunnar and urged him to exhibit his work, not for money, but for needed ego enhancement. Gunnar found that discussing his paintings with someone who saw them with fresh eyes ignited his interest in exhibiting them. For years, he had painted without showing his work publicly. When he did, he was amazed at the intensity of the reactions. Because he had painted with no fear of public exhibition, Gunnar's work exposed his innermost feelings; other artists were reluctant to show such feelings. Within a short time, Gunnar was receiving steady acclaim.

At the same time, Emily, who had all but given up acting, became active in children's theater. Her work was quickly noticed, and other roles were offered her. At this point, Gunnar developed a serious depression. Emily became very concerned and arranged for them to see a therapist.

The therapist who works with a couple in the creative arts must have an affinity for the arts in order to communicate with the clients. With Emily, for example, the therapist cited the character of Nora in *A Doll's House* (Ibsen, 1975) as a model of a woman who subjugates herself to her husband. Gunnar avidly read biographies of artists and copied excerpts or presented books to the therapist to explain his ideas on work. The therapist read these, as well as other books that took an opposite point of view. A visit to his studio, where rooms were crammed with large canvasses of naked bodies filled with torment, revealed more than seeing one or two of his paintings in the office or at an exhibit would have revealed. It also communicated to Gunnar the respect with which the therapist held his work. Finally, it exposed his psyche in ways that months of therapy would not have done.

As Gunnar exhibited more of his work, his depression lifted. Emily took on additional theatrical roles. She discovered that certain roles stretched her personal growth. When such stretching frightened her, she was attracted to a young man. She learned what Gunnar had learned 6 months previously—an artist who draws back from further growth in his or her field considers substitute excitements as a sort of braking effect. The therapist reassured both Emily and Gunnar that, if they plumbed the resources they each already possessed, they would grow in the arts and in their relationship, as well.

The therapist encouraged Gunnar to continue exhibiting his work. It took more courage for Gunnar to develop closer contacts with friends and family in order to feed his need for nurturance. Becoming closer to his friends was a satisfying experience for him, but the idea of developing closeness with his family was very frightening to him. The therapist coached his family-of-origin re-connection through techniques described by Bowen (1978) and Guerin (1976).

The therapist developed four plans, A, B, C, and D, with Gunnar. A bright man, Gunnar was intrigued with the plans and saw them as challenges. He began work on the easiest one, Plan A. By telephone, he arranged a luncheon date with the sister who lived closest to him. He discovered during the luncheon that his sister was not intimidated by their father's success, but found it somewhat tragic that he needed to treat his adult children like inferiors instead of peers.

Plan B required him to telephone the sister who was mildly hostile toward him and tell her he would visit when he was in her area. Once at the meeting, he was to tell her how much he admired her ability to be incisive and ask her for stinging criticism of his work. This strategy was especially frightening for Gunnar, a mild-mannered, easily hurt man. It was planned as a paradox, since it could be expected that being asked to do what she had always done would impede the sister's usual behavior. Gunnar set off on the visit with great trepidation. At his next session, Gunnar was exuberant, an uncommon emotion for him. His sister had confessed her envy of Gunnar, particularly of his ability to stand up to their father.

Gunnar's success with Plans A and B gave him confidence in meeting his third sister and executing Plan C. This sister was the least receptive to his initial overture and, in fact, made no attempt to hide her resentment caused by Gunnar's aloofness toward their father. She refused to meet with him and hung the phone up on him.

The therapist reframed Gunnar's lack of sucess with Plan C as necessary preparation for the completion of Plan D, the major test. Plan D focused on the day Gunnar would launch his new relationship with his father, which was referred to as D Day. This day was to provide Gunnar with the experience of exposing his feelings to the one person he most feared, his father. In preparation, the therapist recommended that Gunnar view the films, *I Never Sang for my Father* and *On Golden Pond*. Both provide good examples of the obstacles to growth an adult's lack of a peer relationship with a parent can create. They portray successful adult children who are still intimidated by their fathers and lack a nurturing relationship with them.

The build-up to Gunnar's meeting with his father was intense. The therapist warned Gunnar that his goals had to be specific and modest. He drew up three of them:

1. His father would hug him.
2. Gunnar would continue talking, regardless of his father's criticism. (Usually he fell silent when his father criticized him.)
3. His father would promise to allow Gunnar to paint his portrait.

The therapist helped Gunnar visualize the meeting by incorporating some precise techniques of Neuro-Linguistic Programming (Bandler & Grinder, 1975; Grinder & Bandler, 1976). The therapist verbally "anchored" an experience that Gunnar remembered from his early life when he and his father laughed together. As Gunnar remembered more frustrating events, the therapist "fired the anchor" so that the good remembrance would overlap the bad. This approach provided Gunnar with positive feelings while he imagined himself in a negative scenario. It gave him additional resources to deal with his father.

On D Day, Gunnar achieved the second and third of his three goals. First, it was easy for Gunnar to keep talking, as his father seemed to relish having Gunnar court him. Only once did Gunnar begin to revert to silence. When he told his father he had received an award for his paintings, his father responded, "Don't take those things seriously. They give awards out so they can get their pictures in the paper." Gunnar recovered and laughed. Second, his father agreed to sit for a portrait and even suggested a date for the occasion. He was very flattered by Gunnar's request and told him he often wondered why Gunnar had not asked him to sit for a portrait.

Gunnar's hope that his father would hug him was not realized at that meeting. The therapist asked Gunnar to sketch his father hugging him. After several unsuccessful attempts, it was apparent to Gunnar that he himself was not ready for his father to hug him. Animosity toward his father lessened as Gunnar's confidence in his work grew, however.

Marital closeness had been impossible as long as Gunnar was afraid to develop an adult relationship with his family of origin. When Gunnar improved his relationship with his family of origin, he and Emily became closer. Fears that they could not discuss sensitive issues were allayed. They spoke about their premarital loves, about parenting experiences, about money, about Emily's mother, and about sex. It was surprising to both Gunnar and Emily that they could differ and grow more intimate simultaneously. Not only had Gunnar been afraid of intimacy, but he had been afraid to own his artistic talents. In effect, he had been a "closet painter."

Emily became aware, with the therapist's help, that she possessed as many fears about dealing with her mother as Gunnar did about dealing with his family. She began reconnective work with her own family of origin.

Because of Gunnar's depression at the time therapy began, it was easier to begin treatment for Gunnar and Emily around his unfulfilled artistic life than to follow a more traditional marital therapy program. The therapist emphasized the skills Gunnar possessed in his work to increase his self-esteem. As a result, Gunnar gained a sense of competence that he was then able to translate into his marriage.

The therapist suspected that Emily and Gunnar were in collusion about the presenting problem. They both suffered from depression caused by avoiding the development of their artistic abilities. As one of them changed, the system changed. It no longer made any sense to either of them to view Emily as perfect and Gunnar as "the problem."

Ludwig and Sarah

Ludwig, a 32-year-old composer, and Sarah, a 31-year-old oil painter, had been married 1 year. Both were married for the first time, although each had had long-term live-in relationships with other people. Ludwig continued to be friends with a woman he had lived with for 4 years. When he spoke of his former relationship, he described the difference between a woman in the arts and one in the sciences: "Deborah was a computer planner who worked from 9 to 5. I would try to finish my work by the time she arrived home. She wanted to eat by 6:30 and go out to the movies or to visit friends. But I might be in the middle of an idea I was playing with. She would tell me I was working too hard. Music is my life. I may struggle with it but I love it. Sarah understands that, because it is the same for her."

Sarah did more of "woman's work" (e.g., laundry, food preparation) than Ludwig did. When she did not, she felt guilty. She saw no problem in spending money on her paints or canvasses, despite the fact that her works had not brought income into the house as yet. Having received a small legacy from her grandmother, Sarah provided a kind of dowry to the household. In fact, when their expenses increased, it was Sarah who worked a few days a week as a temporary secretary.

Ludwig and Sarah expressed great happiness with each other. He believed his work had improved as a result of happiness in his major relationship. Although he was unaware of sexual difficulties related to the ups and downs of his work, Sarah reported that he had less interest in sex when his work was not progressing well.

Both families of this couple were very supportive of the marriage. Sarah said her parents were "glad I'm in love." At one time her mother encouraged her to marry someone who was wealthy and could support her in her art. Now, however, she was happy that Ludwig and Sarah were married.

A therapist called on to work with this young couple should encourage them to sometimes relate as a couple, rather than as two independent entities. They seem likely to pursue individual solutions to problems, a path many couples in the arts take. In this case, a therapist might use metaphors to create a sense of unity. An appropriate metaphor for Ludwig and Sarah would involve sound for him and sight for her. Such a metaphor should enable the couple to envision the future consistent with their art—his in music, hers in painting.

If Sarah began to dedicate herself to Ludwig's comfort, the therapist might ask her to imagine two pictures: (1) a picture of herself in 5 years, perhaps as a stereotypical housewife, tired and working at an uninteresting job; (2) a picture of herself as she would like to be, energetic and a successful painter. Then, the two imaginary pictures would dialogue with one another. Finally, the therapist might ask Ludwig to produce the music for each picture. It would then become apparent that Sarah was being producer, director, writer, actor, and critic; she was not allowing Ludwig to design a role in their marriage. Furthermore, Ludwig was colluding with her to exclude himself from equal status in the relationship. By encouraging Sarah and Ludwig to place their individual imprints on the relationship, the therapist would provide an opportunity for them to experience the joys of shared vision.

On the issue of sex, it would be important again for Sarah and Ludwig to express their individual perceptions of events. Sarah is timid about asserting her needs if she thinks they differ from Ludwig's. The therapist might suggest that Sarah exhibit her work publicly, an experience that would lead to simultaneous criticism and praise. In other words, she would experience rewards and disappointments in the same event. Sarah must also be willing to experience both in sex; she cannot expect rewards only. Her reluctance to exhibit her work has similarities to her timidity in initiating sex. When Ludwig does not make sexual overtures to her, she literally "fades out of the picture."

Jane and Harvey

Jane was a tall, 36-year-old artist with dark hair who had an artistic flair in her dressing. Her 34-year-old husband, Harvey, was a furniture designer and woodworker who looked and dressed like a 1960s hippie; he had long hair and a mustache; was tall and skinny; and wore steel-rimmed glasses, blue jeans, and fringed shirts.

Originally, Jane consulted a therapist because of an obsession she had about her physical health. She and her husband later sought therapy as a couple because Harvey wanted children and Jane was unsure whether she wanted to become a parent. Jane earned most of the couple's money by working in the art department of a city newspaper. She hoped to gain fame as a landscape artist. "I want to go for the big time. He's very comfortable—doing what he enjoys. I have the anger and the drive. 'You've got to do it, you've got to do it.'" Jane and Harvey agreed that Jane's need for recognition was greater than his.

Jane was very glad she married someone in the arts. Harvey "doesn't try to cheer me up. He tells me, 'you've got to work harder.'" She was afraid that, if she had children, she would lose "the edge" that drives people to success. While she took full responsibility for managing the household and providing predictable income and health benefits, she did not feel assured that she could take on the responsibility of motherhood.

Jane and Harvey had separate friends and leisure activities. He liked to play tennis and golf with lifelong friends. She liked to be alone and "talk" with her paintings. She found it a spiritual experience. She and her paintings were bonded, and she would say, "We can do it" or "We're really getting it" to them.

Jane liked to paint at The Academy where she took classes. "There is a certain mood there. The students are all moody. I like that atmosphere." She also enjoyed teaching part-time at The Academy, but did not feel comfortable as a full-fledged authority figure. She enjoyed being a peer to her students. (This is the same problem that Jane had concerning motherhood—she did not want to be the parent, but rather the child.)

Jane had a passion for fantasy. She fantasized a relationship with a rock star and devoted a good deal of time to dreams of their life together. She collected his albums and public relations photographs secretly, as she was ashamed of it.

Harvey played the bass in a combo two nights a week, the same two nights that Jane worked as a paste-up artist at a city newspaper for the morning edition. Harvey explained their relationship, "We don't share in much at all. But as far as love for each other, it's really super." Jane agreed. "We live full lives separately from each other. It's not like this cute, cozy relationship where we're Siamese twins. But we are a couple. I climb into bed with him every night. Some of our friends do everything together; they're like glue. Sometimes I think maybe there's something wrong with us. We may sit on the porch and talk for hours. And then we may go for a few days with very little talk."

In individual therapy sessions with Jane before couple therapy began, the therapist encouraged her fantasizing. It was a paradoxical move based on the fact that in ten years of psychiatric therapy no success in diminishing the fantasy had occurred. Jane painted a very good portrait of the rock star she idolized, but she did not exhibit it for fear doing so would provoke criticism of her. The therapist asked her to describe the life she dreamed of sharing with the rock star and the ways in which she could create such a life for herself. Jane would have to remove the impediments she has placed in her own artistic development.

A large obstacle to Jane's artistic development was the attitude of her family of origin toward her work. Unlike Harvey's family, in which everyone practiced one of the arts either as a skilled amateur or a professional, Jane's family was composed of practical, blue-collar workers. They saw Jane as flighty. Finally, Jane said that her parents thought "Harvey is too good for me."

At that time in Jane's individual therapy, Harvey asked to attend the sessions in order to discuss having a family. Jane disclosed her fear that, if they had a child, she would no longer be Number One with Harvey and then she would be Number One with no one. The therapist asked them to create some mental imagery in which Harvey exerted his talent for socializing by setting up an exhibit of Jane's work. Because they were accustomed to doing everything individually, they seemed to need some experience working as a team. Their cooperative development of the image enabled them to conjure up a picture that was pleasing to both of them. Jane was to imagine herself letting Harvey be part of her dreams. By becoming known in her own right, for her own uniqueness, she would remain Harvey's Number One priority. In this image, Harvey would feel that she needed him and he did not have to create such a solitary life. After developing this mental image into a more detailed picture, Harvey admitted that he fantasized a good deal of the time as well.

Jane and Harvey continue in therapy. They have not yet decided whether to have a baby.

Rima and Sebastian

Rima, a 46-year-old writer, and Sebastian, a 42-year-old potter, were described by friends as "the perfect couple." They had two teen-aged children, a son and a daughter. Like their parents, the children were artistic and articulate.

Rima had been a successful sculptor when she married Sebastian 18 years previously. Her first marriage to a banker ended precipitously after 2 years without producing any children.

When Rima and Sebastian married, they decided to move to the country and raise a family. Their move from New York City required Rima to give up her studio there and, basically, to give up sculpting. After the birth of their second child, she began a new career as a writer.

Sebastian threw museum-quality pots. Yet, when he and Rima began to have children, he took a job as copywriter in a publishing house in order to provide a dependable income for his family. He continued potting and received national awards for his work as the years progressed. Still, he continued work at the publishing house.

Rima and Sebastian considered themselves profeminist, but they did not realize how deeply rooted their traditional values were. Sebastian provided the income for the family, and Rima felt no need to produce money through her work. Sebastian provided.

Things were smooth until Sebastian became 40. He began to question everything and to wonder if his life had been wasted. He attended a seminar dedicated to understanding relationships and became more certain that he was unhappy.

At first, Rima decided to "weather the storm." She believed her marriage would survive this crisis. After all, Sebastian was an excellent father, and there were many things in their life together that they both admitted were satisfying. While some things improved, notably their sex lives, they failed to resolve their basic differences.

In therapy, the clinician recommended that Sebastian work on his relationship with his sister and brother; he did so with zest. The therapist also recommended that Sebastian improve his life-long unsatisfying relationship with his father. It was the one area of his life that contained enormous amounts of anger, and he had addressed that anger only in clay. Finally, Sebastian joined a men's consciousness-raising group and saw a male therapist for individual work. During that time he decided to leave Rima and his children. Rima felt that he had decided to leave years before, but actually gained the courage to do so when he talked with other men.

Rima discovered that she had hidden behind her husband's protectiveness, allowing him to be the major breadwinner. In this way she had obstructed her own growth as an artist and avoided facing herself. When Sebastian left her, Rima submitted some of her poetry for publication and was happy at its acceptance. Although her marriage to Sebastian ended in divorce, Rima believes that the aesthetic life they shared was very satisfying. The men she now dates are also in the arts.

METHODS OF PROVIDING THERAPY

Therapists who work with couples in the arts should (1) present themselves as experts in their own field, (2) learn as much as possible about the respective fields of each member of the couple, (3) map out the problem with the couple, and (4) develop a team approach with the clients to problem solving.

Therapists As Experts

Artists are accustomed to respecting master teachers, conductors, and published authors; in other words, they respect people who demonstrate expertise in their specialty. It is imperative that the couple perceive the therapist as an expert in marital problems, even during the initial interview.

Many issues that arise with couples in the arts center on authority. Artists not only criticize themselves, but also learn to accept criticism from those more knowledgeable than they are. As they become more confident of their artistry, they usually become more discriminating about whom they allow to criticize their work. This may be one of the reasons marriages between persons in the same subspecialty of a field have more problems than do others; the couple may disagree about the authority rights of one another. Who has the right to criticize the other? What gives them the right to criticize? As Harvey described the responses to his wife's request for feedback about her work, "I may hesitate to give her an honest answer because that means serious discussion for the next half hour. She wants specifics, and she wants to know what gives me the right to make such comments." As a result of this attitude, the therapist must speak as an authority on marital relationships, not on art.

Knowledge of the Arts

The usual methods of reading, attending concerts, or viewing art exhibits help therapists to obtain a basic knowledge of client specialties. As the clients' trust in the therapist builds, reading the works of the client-author, attending performances of the client-musician or client-actor, and visiting the studios of client-artist assists the therapeutic process. This not only allows the therapist to appreciate the dedication required to produce art, but also reinforces the client's belief that the therapist respects his or her work.

In a study on the traits of persons in the creative arts and those of psychologists, Loomis (1982) found that creative persons had high scores in introversion and psychologists had high scores in extroversion. It is often difficult for those whose lives have an external focus to develop rapport with those whose lives are so full internally. In order to work effectively with persons in the arts, it is useful for therapists to pursue some artistic discipline. The frustration, as well as the total absorption, inherent in learning to play the piano, in writing a book, or photographing a landscape allow a therapist to capture a glimpse of the artist's world.

Even sitting with an artist as he or she works can be helpful. Often, a visit to the workplace of each member of the couple provides a realistic view of their work lives. Because artists are usually possessive of their space and cannot abide having someone "invade" their studios, it is important that the visiting therapist respect the layout of the room and avoid handling items casually.

To say "that's beautiful" or "that's so lyrical" frequently brings a disclaimer from the artist. Making a personal comment, such as "that really appeals to me" or "I feel so moved by that music," forces the artist to deal with the therapist-commentator as a person rather than as a pseudo-authority on his or her life's work. (It is also a model of what a personal relationship can be.) This is conveyed succinctly by Rogers (1961), who said:

> If I understand you empathically, see you and what you are feeling and doing from your point of view, enter your private world and see it as it appears to you—and still accept you—then this is safety indeed. In this climate you can permit your real self to emerge, and to express itself in varied and novel formings as it relates to the world. (p. 358)

The artist can identify with someone who is an expert in his or her own area, but is curious about an unknown area. The therapist is laying the groundwork for the client to take ownership of his or her talents, as well as to respect his or her everyday needs (e.g., love, caring, tenderness, acknowledgment, sex, and respect).

Problem Map

It is effective to depict the cycle of a marital problem graphically. Occasionally, a circle indicates the repetitious pattern of problem events, as it does with Gunnar and Emily (Figure 1). When this couple examined the map, it became apparent to them that each feared abandonment. When either received attention from the outside world, the other became either depressed or competitive.

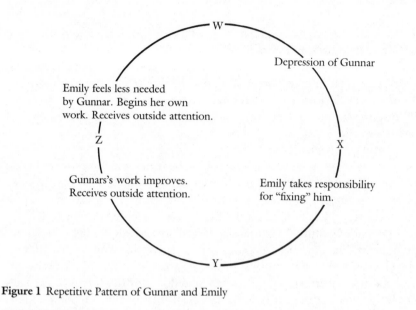

Figure 1 Repetitive Pattern of Gunnar and Emily

Team Approach to Problem Solving

Many artists are accustomed to problem solving, and many marital therapists find artists talented in this arena. When they are asked to join the expert (the therapist) to resolve their own dilemmas, they receive the ultimate support in controlling their own worlds. Their abilities to contribute to problem solutions are respected by an authority figure, and neither spouse is more important than the other.

BENEFITS OF WORKING WITH COUPLES IN THE ARTS

Therapists who work with couples in the arts receive a variety of benefits. First, observation of the techniques used by artists to develop their crafts and the satisfaction that follows such development frequently motivates therapists to pursue their own creative path. Those techniques—total absorption in their work, perseverance despite rejections, and dedication to a long-term goal—can overcome therapists' procrastination about writing or lecturing. Second, the willingness to be flexible and more open to criticism in both their professional and personal lives seems to develop in therapists who work with artists. Finally, attending concerts and art shows, reading books and magazine articles, and becoming aware of the processes behind the production of art all add to a therapist's own life.

CONCLUSION

Although a classic on the marriages of couples in the arts has yet to be written, anecdotal information provides some interesting seminal ideas. For one, the attributes that describe the successful artist (McMullan, 1976) are also the traits mentioned for successful marriage (Hunt, 1982). Those traits—perseverance, high self-esteem, the ability to drop an issue and move on, constructive discontent, detached involvement, disinterested selfishness, and confident humility—are developed over a length of time. Perhaps both good artists and good marriages need time to grow.

"Flexible persistence" (McMullan, 1976) is an especially useful trait in marriage. Flexibility and persistence are often considered opposites, yet to be both flexible and persistent simultaneously is "the core characteristic of the creative individual" (McMullan, 1976, p. 267). Marriage is enhanced by persistently working toward common goals, such as good communication. At the same time, spouses need to be flexible about the paths to those goals.

It is a mistake for a therapist to concentrate on intrapsychic issues when dealing with the marital problems of a couple in the arts. Family-of-origin work or work on professional issues seems more effective. It is important to support them in the development of their individual art, because it is through their art that they develop the full dimension of themselves.

REFERENCES

American Psychiatric Association (1980). *Diagnostic and statistical manual: III.* Washington, DC: Author.

Bandler, R., & Grinder, J. (1975). *The structure of magic.* Palo Alto, CA: Science and Behavior Books.

Bergman, J. (1985). *Fishing for barracuda: Pragmatics of brief systemic therapy.* New York: Norton.

Bowen, M. (1978). *Family therapy in clinical practice.* New York: Jason Aronson.

Grinder, J., & Bandler, R. (1976). *The structure of magic: II.* Palo Alto, CA: Science and Behavior Books.

Guerin, P. (Ed.). (1976). *Family therapy.* New York: Gardner Press.

Hatterer, L. (1965). *The artist in society.* New York: Grove.

Hunt, M.M. (1982). *The universe within: A new science explores the human mind.* New York: Simon and Shuster.

Ibsen, H. (1975). *A doll's house. The wild duck. The lady from the sea.* (R.F. Farquhdrson & E. Marx-Aveling, Trans.). New York: Dutton.

Loomis, M. (1982, January). A new perspective for Jung's typology: The Singer-Loomis inventory of personality. *Journal of Analytical Psychology, 27*(1), 59–69.

McMullan, W.E. (1976). Creative individuals: Paradoxical personages. *The Journal of Creative Behavior, 10*(4), 265–275.

Rogers, C. (1961). *On becoming a person.* New York: Houghton Mifflin.

Rooney, A.A. (1985, March 17). Experience of having name on *New York Times Review of Books* bestseller list. *The New York Times,* VII, 3:1.

Rose, M. (1981, March). *The Vocational Guidance Quarterly,* 236–243.

RECOMMENDED ADDITIONAL READINGS

Amos, S.P. (1978, Aug.). Personality differences between established and less-established male and female creative artists. *Journal of Personality Assessment, 42*(4), 374–377.

Barzun, J., & Graff, H.F. (1985). *The modern researcher* (4th ed.). New York: Harcourt Brace Jovanovich.

Czurles, S.A. (1976). Art creativity vs. spectatoritis. *Journal of Creative Behavior, 10*(2), 104–107.

Hammer, E.F. (1975). Artistic creativity: Giftedness or sickness. *Art Psychotherapy, 2*(2), 173–175.

Helson, R. (1977–1978). Experiences of authors in writing fantasy: Two relationships between creative process and product. *Journal of Altered States of Consciousness, 3*(3), 235–248.

Hopkins, J., & White, P. (1978, July). The dual-career couple: Constraints and supports. *The Family Coordinator,* 253–258.

Isaacs, A.F. (1979, Fall). Creativity in musical composition: How does the composer work? Are insights afforded valuable to other disciplines? *Creative Child and Adult Quarterly, 4*(3), 152–172.

Levi, A.W. (1976, January). The uses of the humanities in personal life. *Journal of Aesthetic Education, 10*(1), 5–17.

Prow, S. (1978, September). Inventing one's own life. *Etudes Psychotherapiques, 33,* 185–189.

Rogers, C. (1980). *A way of being.* New York: Houghton Mifflin.

St. John-Parsons, D. (1978, Fall). Continuous dual-career families: A case study. *Psychology of Women Quarterly, 3*(1), 30–42.

5. Toward a Conceptualization and Treatment of Interfaith Marriage

Nicholas S. Aradi, PhD
Assistant Director
Florida Couples and Family Institute
West Palm Beach, Florida

Traditionally, a faith in common was viewed as a prerequisite for a successful marriage. While a common faith union did not guarantee marital bliss or longevity, it was considered an important ingredient of the socio-cultural glue that held couples together. Interfaith marriage, on the other hand, was perceived as an ill-fated union in which the couple was doomed to a life of spiritual emptiness, marital strife, and eventual divorce.

In spite of the growing trend toward the secularization of the institution of marriage, the declining influence of religion on family structure, and the legitimization of individualistic spirituality (Thornton, 1985), it appears that the adage "the family that prays together, stays together" still applies today. Numerous studies indicate that a similarity of religious upbringing is a reliable predictor of marital adjustment (Bahr & Chadwick, 1985; Filsinger & Wilson, 1984; Hansen, 1981; Schumm, Bollman, & Jurich, 1982). Other studies report (1) higher levels of marital happiness in religiously homogenous marriages than in religiously heterogenous marriages (Alston, McIntosh, & Wright, 1976), (2) a negative effect of religious heterogomy on marital stability (Bumpass & Sweet, 1972), and (3) higher divorce rates for mixed-faith marriages than for same-faith marriages (Landis, 1949; Moller, 1975).

These patterns, coupled with an increase in interfaith marriages over the past 30 years (Glenn, 1982), have important implications for the marital therapist. The research suggests that interfaith couples are a unique, growing, and high-risk population that requires special attention in terms of conceptualization and treatment. Currently, however, there is no specific model to help therapists conceptualize and treat this population.

DEFINITION

In most studies of interfaith marriage in the United States, religious heterogomy is defined as marriage between individuals from two of the three basic Western religions—Protestant, Catholic, and Jewish (Glenn, 1982). Intrafaith differences are rarely studied, because such distinctions are difficult to make, subjective, and not amenable to the research process. For the purposes of understanding the effect of religious differences on marital viability, a finer distinction needs to be made. Consequently, for clinical purposes, interfaith marriage is defined as a union in which one or both spouses, or their family of origin, perceive(s) the other's religion as so significantly different from their own as to create distress. According to this phenomenological view, a couple from basically similar religions (e.g., Southern and American Baptist, Orthodox and Conservative or Reform Jewish), may represent an interfaith marriage if (1) the partner(s) or member(s) of their family of origin perceive(s) a religious mismatch and (2) the mismatch is a source of distress.

BEYOND AN OPPOSING FORCES MODEL OF MARITAL VIABILITY

To help explain what brings and keeps interfaith couples together, it is useful to begin by conceptualizing the determinants of marital viability in general. One approach to the understanding of marital viability is through an extension of the concept of group and marital cohesiveness described by Levinger (1965). According to Levinger, group cohesiveness is the total field of forces that cause members to remain in the group. If the married couple is considered a two-person group, marital cohesiveness is the total field of forces that act on the individuals to keep each one a member of the pair (Levinger, 1965). The degree of cohesiveness is determined by three different forces: (1) positive attractions, (2) negative attractions, and (3) barriers. The combination of these forces yields an area of "interpersonal overlap" that determines the viability of the marital relationship. The greater the overlap, the more cohesive and viable the relationship.

The definition of marital cohesiveness provided by Levinger (1965) appears to be linear and reductionistic, as it suggests that outside forces act on the individual and determine the strength of the couple relationship. A potentially more useful and complete definition, one consistent with current systemic interpretations of couple relationships, is needed to account for reciprocal influences between the individuals, between the couple and their surroundings, and between each individual and his or her surroundings. In addition, rather than forces, the reciprocal influences can be considered energy in the form of information that has meaning and function for the couple's connectedness. From this perspective, marital cohesion can be defined in terms of the total amount of information that functions to maintain and promote the system.

System-generating messages exist on several levels, including intrapsychic (e.g., positive projection process), interpersonal (e.g., mutually satisfying sexual relationship), familial (e.g., mutual acceptance between partner and family of origin), communal (e.g., involvement with friends, organizations), and sociocultural (e.g., shared values and life styles). These messages may also take the form of individual, interpersonal, familial, or extrafamilial rules that maintain the couple system. For example, a strong familial prohibition of divorce is a rule that may constitute a system-generating message.

Conversely, system-degenerating messages function to jeopardize the viability of the couple system. Like system-generating messages, these messages exist on multiple levels. On the familial level, for example, a cross-generational coalition against a spouse may threaten the marital system. These messages may also take the form of rules (e.g., "We must not disagree.").

The extent to which information is system-generating or system-degenerating is determined largely by the level of shared meaning within the couple system, and between the couple system and other system levels. The greater the shared meaning and agreement between the couple, and between the couple and other systems (i.e., family of origin, community), the more system-generating the message. From this framework, interfaith marriage can be viewed as a source of information, albeit a potential system-(dis)organizing class of information, that influences marital viability.

ATTRACTIONS, MOTIVATIONS, AND RELIGIOSITY: THE INDIVIDUAL LEVEL

In treatment, individuals in interfaith marriages must explore the religio-ethnic qualities that initially attracted them to each other. Whether due to rebellion against family mores, curiosity about uniqueness, or a move toward separation and autonomy, the attraction during courtship may have been the other's differences. During the course of the marriage, however, the differences that were once considered virtues may be seen as vices. For example, a Protestant person may seem cool, rational, and able to handle stress with an outwardly calm demeanor, whereas a Jewish person may seem warm, intense, and emotional. Once these two are married, the Protestant's style of resolving problems by patient, methodical analysis may seem intolerable to the Jewish person, who perceives it as distancing and uncaring. On the other hand, the Jewish person's immediate, emotionally intense approach may be overwhelming, chaotic, and threatening to the Protestant spouse, who perceives emotional displays as an expression of dissatisfaction with the relationship. Techniques aimed at reframing such vices as virtues and highlighting the value of the complementarity are part of the therapeutic process in treating interfaith couples (Florence Kaslow, personal communication, 1986).

Assessment of each individual's motivation for marrying outside his or her religion often flows naturally from the examination of attractions. Rarely is there a single reason for marrying outside one's faith; rather, motives tend to be multiple, complex, and often unconscious (Sager, 1976). Some individuals seek a rebalance in the traits of their own religious background (McGoldrick & Preto, 1984). They may be attempting to move away from values and aspects of their religious identity that they dislike by moving toward those that they like. Others may seek to solve family issues. For example, they may be attempting to detriangulate from intense emotional relationships, to obtain revenge for perceived injustices, or to change an ossified, lifeless family system. Assessment of their motivation and expectations for the future is critical in planning and guiding treatment.

The last major area requiring examination on the individual level is religiosity. A widely cited, well-operationalized schema of religiosity was developed by Glock (1962). His model yielded five distinct dimensions of religious commitment:

1. ideological (i.e., beliefs)
2. ritualistic (i.e., practice)
3. experiential (i.e., religious experience or feelings)
4. intellectual (i.e., knowledge of church dogma or scripture)
5. consequential (i.e., religious effects on secular life)

Each dimension represents a different mode of religious expression. Combined, they indicate an individual's overall level of religiosity.

Using this model, the marital therapist is able to break down religiosity into discernible and measurable components. A thorough exploration of each dimension makes it possible to assess the nature and salience of religiosity for each individual and the impact of that religiosity on the couple system. The therapist may ask each partner to explore specific aspects of each dimension through such questions as the following:

1. *ideological:* What are your religious beliefs? How important are they to you? To what extent should your partner share your beliefs?

2. *ritualistic:* Describe your religious practices. How important is it for you to be able to practice your faith? To what extent should your partner practice as you do?
3. *experiential:* Describe your religious experiences or feelings. How important is it for you to strive for and attain religious experiences? To what extent should your partner have the same or similar religious experiences that you do?
4. *intellectual:* Describe the nature and extent of your knowledge of religious doctrine. How important is it for you to have an understanding of scriptures and/or religious dogma? To what extent should your partner have the same religious knowledge that you do?
5. *consequential:* Describe the effect that your religion has on your everyday life. How important is it for religion to permeate your secular life? To what extent should your partner's religious-secular life be like yours?

In addition, the therapist may ask the following questions for each component:

- What will you provide, and what do you expect your partner to provide regarding this area?
- Ideally, how would this aspect of religion be expressed in your relationship?

Each partner's attractions, motives, and religiosity represent the main building blocks of their religious compatibility. The extent to which they match largely determines the (dis)organizing function that interfaith marriage plays in their lives.

RELIGIOUS COMPATIBILITY: THE COUPLE LEVEL

If religiosity is conceptualized broadly as information with system-(dis)organizing functions, religious compatibility can be viewed more specifically as information with system-organizing or system-generating functions. That is, as compatibility between system components increases, so does system organization and viability.

Religious compatibility of interfaith couples consists of four different, yet related, components:

1. comparative level of religiosity
2. level of tolerance for differences
3. mutual expectations
4. ability to create a unique and mutually satisfying religious expression

To determine compatibility at the couple level, the therapist first uses the data obtained during the individual assessment to examine the first three components of compatibility. In evaluating the data, the therapist should address the following sets of questions:

1. How important is religion in each partner's life? How (dis)similar are they regarding the importance of religion?
2. What is each partner's level of tolerance for differences? How (dis)similar are they regarding their tolerance for differences? How skilled is the couple in negotiating differences and arriving at mutually satisfying decisions?
3. What is each partner's expectation of the other regarding religion? How well matched are their expectations?

In general, the greater the difference between the partners, the less probable the pairing and the greater their difficulty in establishing a successful relationship (McGoldrick & Preto, 1984). In addition, (1) the higher *both* partners' level of tolerance for differences, (2) the more skilled they are in negotiating differences, and (3) the more accurate *both* partners' expectations of each other, the greater their potential for religious compatibility. Conversely, the lower the level of tolerance in *either* partner, the less skilled they are in negotiating, and the less accurate *either* partner's expectations of the other, the greater the potential for religious *in*compatibility.

As this pattern suggests, religious compatibility is a potentially tenuous relationship attribute. Because an interfaith relationship requires tolerance; effective negotiation skills; and accurate, mutually acceptable expectations by both partners, it becomes increasingly difficult to attain as the level of religiosity of either partner increases. Often, this is due to the fact that, in most religions, intolerance for differences, especially differences in family members, increases as adherence to higher levels of orthodoxy increases.

RELIGIOUS COMPATIBILITY: BEYOND THE COUPLE LEVEL

While examinations of religiosity on the individual and couple levels are primary in assessing and treating interfaith couples, at least two additional levels should be examined to obtain a more complete picture of a couple's religious compatibility: the extended family and the community. The reaction of the couple's parents and of other significant family members to the interfaith marriage can often make the difference between a marriage that is enduring, enriching, and satisfying, and a marriage that is characterized by isolation, despair, conflict, and eventual divorce. There are at least two key interrelated issues in understanding the relationship between the families of origin and the religious compatibility of interfaith couples: (1) the level of caring and connectedness between parents and offspring, and (2) the level of the parents' acceptance of the interfaith relationship. Generally, the more positively connected the parent-offspring relationship, the more important the parents' acceptance and support of the marriage.

In families that value religious identity, emotional issues inevitably arise as the prospect of intermarriage becomes real. Parents often perceive their child's desire to marry someone outside their faith not only as a threat to the survival of their faith, but also as a rejection or abandonment of the family. Parental negative reactions range from a covert lack of permission and an overt refusal to recognize the marriage to the banishment and symbolic death of the offspring. In treating interfaith couples, the therapist must ascertain the meaning of and reaction to the intermarriage of the respective families of origin in order to facilitate the resolution of emotional issues. This is critical; the greater the support available from both families, the greater the chances of a successful intermarriage. It is important to keep in mind, however, that a family's acceptance and support generally develop gradually and are often tested during life cycle transitions.

In the couple's social network and community contacts, the key variable is the degree of pressure to conform to a particular mode of religious expression. Generally, the more religiously homogeneous and traditional the community, the less support and fewer models available to facilitate and affirm the couple's development of a unique interfaith life style. While living in a religiously heterogeneous and nontraditional community does not guarantee a successful interfaith marriage, it does provide greater latitude and potential for religious diversity, experimentation, and creativity—conditions that support and foster nontraditional religious expression.

INTERFAITH MARRIAGE AND THE LIFE CYCLE

The system-(dis)organizing functions of religion vary over the life cycle for both intrafaith and interfaith couples. For many intrafaith couples, religion has a system-organizing function, as it represents a preexisting, well-defined social structure that provides support and guidance through the course of the family's development. Interfaith couples lack this preexisting structure. Consequently, in addition to working through the usual issues and problems associated with forming a new family system, interfaith couples must create their own religious structure. More specifically, their challenge is to create a unique, mutually satisfying religious expression that will serve them throughout the life cycle. The stages of the family life cycle described by McGoldrick and Carter (1982) can be adapted to illustrate the developmental issues that confront interfaith couples and the tasks required to resolve them (Table 1).

Several conditions are necessary for a couple to develop and maintain a successful interfaith marriage. First, the individuals must become aware of and acknowledge the aspects of their religious background that they value. Second, they must bring forth their dearly held beliefs and rituals, and together they must meld them into one unique, mutually satisfying religious expression. Finally, they must negotiate continuously around their differences and create a religious expression that supports and guides them through life's vicissitudes. For many couples, this is a dynamic, lifelong process that is often fraught with intense frustration and conflict that propels them to seek professional help.

INTERFAITH COUPLES THERAPY

The issues, challenges, and problems that confront interfaith couples are numerous, diverse, and complex. Consequently, the therapist who treats such a couple must use a highly integrative approach (Aradi & Kaslow, 1987) that draws from a broad range of knowledge and skills. At the very least, the therapist must have an understanding of the roles and functions of the institution of religion; the dogma and rituals of specific faiths; intrapsychic, interpersonal, and extended family system levels; and family life cycle theory. The specific skills required to treat interfaith couples include nonjudgmental clarification and interpretation of projections and introjects, assessment of extended family structure and relationships, reframing, restructuring, and communication and negotiation training.

> Phil and Judy were a college-educated couple in their early 30's. They had been married for 6 years, and it was the first marriage for both. The couple had no children, but Judy was 7 months pregnant. Phil was a junior executive with a major insurance company, while Judy was a middle school learning disabilities teacher. Phil reported his religious preference as Catholic; Judy indicated hers as Jewish. Neither practiced their faith, however. Both partners reported marital discord as the reason for seeking therapy. Phil's written comments on the intake form read: "We're constantly fighting. We argue over the smallest things. We can't even agree on what to name our baby. It's become intolerable over the past 6 months." Judy was more specific in writing: "My husband is becoming more and more distant and preoccupied with work. At a time when I need him most, he is

Table 1 Stages of the Interfaith Family Life Cycle

Life Cycle Stages	Issues	Tasks
Courtship	Explore and test religious compatibility.	Share level of religiosity. Begin acceptance, accommodation of religious differences. Share expectations of interfaith marriage. Enlist support/acceptance of family of origin. Begin negotiation of interfaith marriage ceremony.
Marriage	Create interfaith marriage ceremony.	Achieve mutual agreement on ceremony. Have both families in attendance. Seek support and acceptance of both families.
Newlyweds	Develop interfaith couple identity.	Begin expression of unique religion, drawing from each partner's background (e.g., celebration of religious holidays). Maintain contact with both families.
Family with young children	Develop interfaith family identity.	Agree on birth ritual. Agree on nature and extent of religious instruction for children. Foster development of child(ren)'s religious identity based on both parents' backgrounds.
Family with adolescents	Increase religious flexibility.	Allow religious experimentation.
Launching of children	Reexamine and modify religious expression.	Accept and support offspring's choice of religious expression and of mate. Integrate new family.
Later life	Review and refocus religious life.	Accept increased focus on spirituality. Resolve existential issues. Agree on death rituals.

least available. I know I get upset a lot, but I don't know how else to reach him.'' Neither partner reported a history of previous therapy, nor was there any indication of chronic medical problems or substance abuse.

Clinical Impressions and Implications: Developmentally, the couple is at a major life cycle transition. Explore religious difference.

Initially, the couple were seen together to gather additional data. The couple agreed that, except for "some trying moments around the wedding," their relationship had been satisfying until recently. Efforts to obtain a clear picture of the couple's relationship before the present crisis were unsuccessful, as both individuals were eager to prove to the therapist how unfairly they had been treated by their spouse. The essence of Judy's complaints focused on her feeling that Phil had grown distant and inattentive toward her and had become overly involved and obsessed by his work. Her tearful account of Phil's neglect was punctuated by a passive, helpless demeanor. As Judy spoke, Phil squirmed and appeared agitated, periodically rolling his eyes and shaking his head in disbelief. It was necessary on several occasions to block Phil from interrupting and taking issue with Judy's account. When she had finished, Judy was asked what she hoped to accomplish in therapy. She stated that she wanted the fighting to stop and for Phil to be more supportive and involved.

The focus then turned to Phil. Asked to describe the problem from his point of view, his immediate reaction, once again, was to refute his wife's account and accuse her of being demanding and dependent. Consequently, the therapist had to deflect Phil's recriminations by acknowledging his dissatisfaction, assuring him that he would get an opportunity to react to his wife's story, and redirect his focus to the description of the problem as he saw it. Phil's main complaint had to do with changes he perceived in his wife. He said that she had become irritable, critical, and dependent lately. He understood that he had to be more helpful and more available now that she was pregnant, but her constant demands and criticism repelled him. When asked what he hoped to gain from therapy, he stated, "I want it to be like it was before— peaceful and no fighting. I want her to be like she was before— easygoing, self-sufficient, and supportive of me."

Phil's identification of his goals in therapy naturally led into another area of exploration, "What attracted you to your partner?" After thinking about the question for some time, Phil began by describing his background: "I come from a strict, formal, quite religious family. There were rules about everything, and it seemed that almost everything that was fun was also a sin. Judy was, I guess, liberating." As he spoke, Phil softened and his shrill tone became warm and soothing. "She was fun-loving, spontaneous . . . and didn't seem to have a sense of guilt about anything. She believed in me and made me feel I was good." In a faltering voice, he added, "We really loved each other in those days."

Turning to Judy to ask what attracted her to Phil, the therapist could see her posture, too, had changed. With shoulders less constricted and hands loosely folded on her lap, she began to describe her reasons for marrying Phil. "Besides finding him physically attractive, he seemed so strong, so solid. He always seemed to know what to do, to make decisions without a hassle. No arguing, no outbursts, no tension. Cool and in control. Very different from what I was used to."

Clinical Impressions and Implications: Adequate level of commitment to marriage appears to be present. Each appears to have sought something in the other that was missing in the family of origin and that would make him or her complete/happy. Explore more fully motivations to marry and family of origin of each spouse.

A total of six sessions, consisting of both individual and couple sessions, were conducted to assess each person's conscious and unconscious expectations and motivations, sociocultural background, and relative religiosity. It was revealed that Judy was the younger of two girls from an intact, middle-class, urban Jewish family. Her sister, Rochelle, was 7 years older than she, which made Judy often feel like an only child. Her father was a retired sales representative who had been away on business trips during most of Judy's childhood and adolescence. She described him as a man who, "whether he was home or not, was never really there. He was a quiet man who never wanted to disturb the waters. It was so frustrating; whenever I wanted him to make a decision, it was always, 'go ask your mother.' He never took a stand on anything in the house. I wish just once he had stood up to her. She ran the house." Judy went on to describe her mother as a basically well-meaning, but lonely, woman who seemed to live through her daughters, particularly through Judy. "She was involved in all aspects of our lives—school, friends, boyfriends, everything! And it got worse when Rochelle went away to college. It was like she had to know and be involved in everything. My father saw it, but couldn't do anything. Whenever he'd ask her to leave me alone, she'd lay into him about what a negligent husband and father he was and how he had no right to criticize since he was never home. When we disagreed, it usually ended up with me and my mother screaming at each other and my father walking out. By the end of high school and all through college we'd fight, and I would usually end up doing what I wanted— except the decision about college. I still regret not having gone away to school." Judy added that part of her was unsure of being able to make it alone, away from home.

The family was described as moderately religious. They observed the high holy days, and both girls had been bat mitzvahed. Judy described her religiosity as primarily "a cultural and family thing, not really religious in the strict sense." A closer examination of her family's religiosity revealed relatively low experiential and intellectual expression, moderate ideological expression, and relatively high ritualistic and consequential expression. This meant that, from her recollection, there was little emphasis either on striving for and experiencing religious/spiritual feelings or on studying and understanding religious dogma. Judy stated that there was some emphasis on knowing and expressing her religious beliefs in her family (intellectual expression), but she was not sure how important this was. "I don't know what my religious beliefs are, except that I believe in God. The rest is not that important to me." Most of Judy's Jewish identity evolved from a modicum of religious practice (i.e., ritualistic) and its impact on everyday life (i.e., consequential). "What I enjoyed most growing up was celebrating religious holidays with the family. It's a tradition I hope to continue with our family."

The ritualistic and consequential aspects of Judy's religious upbringing had continued to hold significance and had been an area of conflict since her marriage. Disagreement first emerged when she announced her engagement. Although her parents and sister liked Phil, Judy always felt that they had tacitly disapproved because he was not Jewish. The most overt disapproval came from her mother, who persisted in advising her "not to rush into anything" and to "think of how it will affect the family." At first, Judy had not understood what her mother meant, but she quickly found out once the announcement was made. Her grandmother openly disapproved of her marrying a "goy," and several relatives refused to attend the wedding, presumably in protest.

The wedding ceremony itself was a source of conflict for the couple and their respective families. Initially, Judy had envisioned a "highly reform" Jewish ceremony. Phil strongly opposed the idea, however. Even though he had "left the Church" many years ago and no longer considered himself a practicing Catholic, Phil was surprised to find himself opposing Judy's plans for the wedding and advocating a spiritually and ritualistically more familiar ceremony. He explained, "While I still find much of the Church's dogma stifling and pretty irrelevant, I guess I still identify with the Church." Phil went on to describe his religious upbringing as quite strict and formal. Unlike those of his wife, Phil's ideological, intellectual, and ritualistic religious expressions were quite pronounced. Through 12 years of parochial school, Phil had developed a clear, well-defined set of religious beliefs; understood fully the Church's rules and precepts; and dutifully practiced his faith (i.e., daily prayer and mass, weekly confession and Holy Communion). Although religious training and practice had been a consistent part of Phil's upbringing, their experiential and consequential effects had been minimal. Phil stated that he did not remember ever being particularly moved or inspired by religion, nor did he feel that his religion had any particularly far-reaching effects on other aspects of his life. Rather, for Phil, religion was compartmentalized. "Going to church or studying the catechism was just one of the many things we did each day. When it was over, it was over, like anything else. It didn't seem to affect other parts of our lives."

Phil's family background was also different from Judy's. He was the oldest of five children, and both parents worked. His father was an accountant for the city, and his mother taught ninth-grade English. Phil described his parents as hard-working, formal, and emotionally unexpressive. He rarely saw his parents show affection toward one another. Furthermore, although Phil felt that they loved their children, his parents did not seem to have enough time to spend with the children. Since both parents worked, he had been given the responsibility of caring for his siblings. Phil stated, "Between school and caring for the kids, growing up was hard work, not much fun. But things changed when I went to college. Two things happened. I took some philosophy courses and started questioning my religion. And, later, I met Judy and began to enjoy myself and have fun."

Clinical Impressions and Implications: Judy's motives for marrying appear to include disengagement from family of origin, attainment of qualities that were missing in family of origin (e.g., strong, decisive male figure), and alleviation of the anxiety of being on her own. Phil's motives were somewhat different and included attainment of intimacy, permission to have fun and be spontaneous, and rebellion from an overly formal and emotionally barren family atmosphere. Both spouses demonstrate some identification with their respective faiths; this appears to be a source of disagreement.

Because Judy and Phil were in a symmetrical interaction characterized by blame and criticism, the therapist restricted them from communicating directly with each other. All communication was channeled through the therapist, who attempted to break this pattern by normalization, reframing, and communication skill training. The therapist told the couple that their relationship appeared to have a sound foundation, but their regard for each other had begun to erode over the years. This erosion accelerated with Judy's pregnancy and the stressors that accompanied it. The message continued: "Many of the conflicts you are having are common and can be solved if caught in time. The two of you seem to care enough about your relationship to work on these problems while they are still manageable." Then the therapist informed them that part of their treatment would consist of learning to talk to each other in a way that prevented or minimized conflict (Guerney, 1977).

Several themes and key issues emerged during the process of communication skill training. Examination of the cause and evolution of Judy's initial dissatisfaction with Phil's emotional distance and preoccupation with work revealed that this approach to life was one of the qualities that initially attracted her. In fact, during the planning of their wedding, it was Phil's cool, logical demeanor that helped calm Judy through several emotional outbursts with her mother. This same quality had now become a source of distress, however. Consequently, Phil's emotional detachment was reframed as an attempt to demonstrate the stability and support that she admired and valued. Since it no longer proved useful, Phil was directed to ask and discuss—"How else could he provide stability and support so that it would be useful?"

On the surface, Phil's primary dissatisfaction was Judy's "constant nagging and wanting to be with me." A brief positive interpretation of the behavior as "Judy possibly wanting more closeness and sharing" seemed to hit home as Phil revealed that this was one of the qualities that had first attracted him to Judy. "She had a way of drawing me out and making me express things I wouldn't tell anyone else. I could be emotional with her without feeling ashamed or weak." Phil was directed to discuss with his wife ways that she could try to be intimate with him that he would not perceive as nagging. Also explored were ways in which Phil could become more aware of his own needs for intimacy and could initiate closeness with his wife.

As the couple began to communicate more openly and respectfully, the issues changed from immediate, conflict-producing problems to more protracted and preconscious sources of conflict. Religious differences became the unifying theme of the remainder of therapy. Mutual resentment over the wedding was the first substantive indication that the couple had suppressed their personal needs for religious expression and had not made progress in developing a unique, jointly satisfying religious expression. Each spouse felt that he or she had "given in" to the other in certain areas in order to avoid confrontation, conflict, and possible breakup. The result was that both partners felt that "something was missing" in the wedding, and something was missing in their present relationship.

Both Phil and Judy appeared to have some significant, although somewhat different, needs for religion in their lives, but few attempts at identifying, clarifying, and communicating their needs had been made. The effects of this avoidance were discussed. Resulting problems ranged from mild dissatisfaction (e.g., a free-floating sense of emptiness) to more focused distress (e.g., resentment of the spouse). A recurrence and exacerbation of the problems were predicted with the birth of the child, since both events (i.e., marriage and birth) represent life cycle transitions that have religious implications. With the impending birth, however, "a rare opportunity to address this issue" was at hand.

Relying particularly on expressive and empathic skills (Guerney, 1977), the couple began to address fundamental questions concerning their religious beliefs and the role that religion should play in their lives. Essentially, what emerged was some disagreement over dogma, but a mutual respect for differences. Neither spouse expressed a need to adhere strictly to his or her doctrine; instead, they discovered that they agreed on a set of moral principles that underlie their faiths. As parents, they believed that they could teach these principles themselves, rather than have their child attend formal religious classes. The couple agreed to expose their child equally to both religions, as they viewed such contact as broadening and enriching. This exposure would occur through contact with grandparents and other relatives. Since each spouse valued ritualistic expression, achieving an agreement on this issue was more difficult. If a religious holiday was important to one spouse, it was agreed that they would celebrate it together. The issue of participation in rituals was more sensitive, as both spouses strongly valued certain ones. Complete agreement in this area was not reached, but a tentative guideline that major home-based rituals (e.g., Passover and Easter dinners, Christmas and Chanukah) would be observed and practiced to the degree defined by the more invested spouse was established. Regarding formal religious (i.e., church-/temple-based) ceremonies, the less interested spouse would accept and support the partner's expression, but could choose to not participate.

Clinical Impressions and Implications: Couple appear to have developed sufficient mastery of skills to begin to solve their own problems. With the amelioration of the presenting problems and their improved ability to work through differences, couple is showing eagerness to terminate therapy. Issues still remaining: communicating couple's religious expression to their respective families, anticipating negative reactions and exploring responses, and anticipating difficulties during life cycle transitions (e.g., birth of child).

The therapist supported the couple's efforts at working together to develop a mutually satisfying religious expression. It was emphasized that their work had just begun and that they represented one of those unique couples who must continuously create their own "family faith." They were shown a diagram illustrating the family life cycle and the specific tasks required to negotiate each transition successfully. The couple were asked to brainstorm ways in which they might approach each future task. Finally, they were asked when and how they were going to share their evolving faith with their family. Phil was eager to tell his family the next time they were together. Judy appeared more cautious, expressing a need to "try it out for a while first" and internalize it before talking about it with her family.

Clinical Impressions and Implications: The reversal (i.e., Phil's eager spontaneity and Judy's methodical cautiousness) was encouraging, as it appeared to indicate a greater range of behaviors for both partners. Also noteworthy was the couple's respect for each other's differences in telling their respective families.

CONCLUSION

The therapist who treats interfaith couples must possess a solid understanding of the different dimensions of religious expression (Glock, 1962) and their effect on the individual, couple, and extended family subsystems over the life cycle. In terms of process, the assessment of the individuals on each dimension, work on couple incongruence, and facilitation of compatibility represent key therapeutic stages. Because of the particularly sensitive and personal nature of this topic, the therapist should possess a high degree of tolerance for differences, a nonjudgmental attitude, and clarity and security about personal religious beliefs. The therapist's ability to maintain such a stance is often tested while treating interfaith couples, because these clients tend to be rigid in their thinking, opinionated, and proselytizing. Finally, the therapist must keep in mind that religious incompatibility is rarely the presenting problem for interfaith couples. Rather, it tends to emerge gradually in therapy as a major underlying source of conflict when the presenting problems abate.

REFERENCES

Alston, J., McIntosh, W.A., & Wright, L.M. (1976). Extent of interfaith marriages among white Americans. *Sociological Analysis, 37*, 261–264.

Aradi, N., & Kaslow, F. (1987). Theory integration in family therapy: Definition, rationale, content, and process. *Psychotherapy, 24*, 595–608.

Bahr, H.M., & Chadwick, B.A. (1985). Religion and family in Middletown U.S.A. *Journal of Marriage and the Family, 47*, 407–414.

Bumpass, L., & Sweet, J. (1972). Differentials in marital instability: 1970. *American Sociological Review, 37*, 754–766.

Filsinger, E., & Wilson, M.R. (1984). Religiosity, socioeconomic rewards, and family development: Predictors of marital adjustment. *Journal of Marriage and the Family, 46*, 663–670.

Glenn, N.D. (1982). Interreligious marriage in the United States: Patterns and recent trends. *Journal of Marriage and the Family, 44*, 555–566.

Glock, C. (1962, May-June). On the study of religious commitment. *Religious Education*, pp. 98–110.

Guerney, B. (1977). *Relationship enhancement therapy.* San Francisco: Jossey-Bass.

Hansen, G.L. (1981). Marital adjustment and conventionalization: A reexamination. *Journal of Marriage and the Family, 43*, 855–863.

Kaslow, F.W. (1987). Personal communication.

Landis, J.T. (1949). Marriages of mixed and non-mixed religious faith. *American Sociological Review, 14*, 401–407.

Levinger, G. (1965). Marital cohesiveness and dissolution: An integrative review. *Journal of Marriage and the Family, 27*, 19–28.

McGoldrick, M., & Carter, E. (1982). The family life cycle. In F. Walsh (Ed.), *Normal family process* (pp. 167–195). New York: Guilford Press.

McGoldrick, M., & Preto, N. (1984). Ethnic intermarriage: Implications for therapy. *Family Process, 3*, 347–364.

Moller, A.S. (1975). Jewish-Gentile divorce in California. *Jewish Social Studies, 37*, 279–290.

Sager, C. (1976). *Marriage contracts and couples therapy*. New York: Brunner/Mazel.

Schumm, W.R., Bollman, S.R., & Jurich, A.P. (1982). The marital conventionalization argument: Implications for the study of religiosity and marital satisfaction. *Journal of Psychology and Theology, 10*, 236–241.

Thornton, A. (1985). Reciprocal influences of family and religion in a changing world. *Journal of Marriage and the Family, 47*, 381–394.

6. "Bulimic" Couples: Dynamics and Treatment

Paula Levine, PhD
Director
Anorexia and Bulimia Resource Center
Coral Gables, Florida

B ulimia is a complex eating disorder characterized by recurrent episodes of binge eating followed by some form of purging, such as self-induced vomiting, laxative or diuretic abuse, and fasting, often in combination with strenuous exercise. While the *Diagnostic and Statistical Manual of Mental Disorders (DSM III)* of the American Psychiatric Association (1980) does not specifically require self-induced vomiting for a diagnosis of bulimia, the term *bulimia* is almost always used to define the binge-purge syndrome. Other identifying features of the condition include the rapid consumption of large quantities of high-calorie food during the binge; fear of loss of control while eating; extreme fluctuations in weight; and feelings of depression, self-deprecation, and guilt.

The physical effects of bulimia are usually reversible when the bingeing-purging stops. Bulimia can have serious complications, however, such as electrolyte imbalances, swollen salivary glands, dental deterioration, and chronic gastrointestinal disturbances. Bulimia can even be fatal, usually because the patient's continuous vomiting and/or extreme laxative abuse has produced a potassium deficit that leads to cardiac arrest.

The binge-purge cycle typically begins during adolescence or young adulthood, although it sometimes begins later in life. Many bulimics are perfectionistic and achievement-oriented; some are also addicted to drugs or alcohol. Bulimia occurs predominantly in females. Evidence collected in the past 15 years suggests that the prevalence of eating disorders among young women is increasing dramatically (Bruch, 1973; Casper, 1983; Halmi, Falk, & Schwartz, 1981; Pyle, Mitchell, & Eckert, 1981). In studies of normal college populations, it has been found that 13% of 355 students surveyed (Halmi et al., 1981) and 4.1% of 1,355 students surveyed (Pyle et al., 1981) met the *DSM III* diagnostic criteria for bulimia. Because bulimia has become almost epidemic on some college campuses and because eating disorders in general are occurring more frequently in older women (Garfinkel & Garner, 1982), more and more bulimics who seek treatment are likely to be married.

THE "BULIMIC" COUPLE

While a great deal has been written about family therapy and group therapy for bulimics, only a handful of articles have focused on couples therapy for bulimics (Foster, 1986; Madanes, 1981; Schwartz, Barrett, & Saba, 1985). One reason for this gap in the literature may be that, despite a bulimic's marital status, most eating disorder programs offer individual, family, or group therapy programs as their primary treatment modalities; marital therapy is generally offered only as an adjunct to the patient's therapy once the symptom has been controlled.

Another possible reason for the dearth of literature on marital therapy for patients with eating disorders is that very little is known about the function of bulimia within the marriage. Despite the increasing frequency of bulimia in older women, marital conflict as a primary cause of bulimia is decidedly infrequent. Few bulimics report that they started bingeing and purging while married (Boskind-White & White, 1983); thus it appears that marital relationship issues may contribute to the maintenance and exacerbation of bulimic symptoms, but rarely cause them. The bulimia often becomes the focus of much of the couple's interactions, however. Because bulimic behaviors are particularly susceptible to stress, heightened marital conflict often increases the frequency of symptoms. In this way, the wheel may continue around and around, until some form of intervention takes place.

A few authors have recently addressed the dynamics and treatment of the bulimic couple as a unit. Madanes (1981) described symptomatic behavior in one spouse as a solution, albeit an unfortunate one, to the power struggle in the marriage. In her view, the symptoms are maintained in order to change the hierarchical arrangement and balance the division of power in the couple. One of two hierarchical incongruities results: (1) the bulimic assumes an inferior position, and the nonbulimic assumes the superior position of helper; or (2) the bulimic refuses to be helped, rendering the nonbulimic helpless and thus elevating the bulimic to a superior position. Madanes was convinced that the interaction around the bulimic's symptoms becomes a metaphor for other marital issues that the couple deny.

To illustrate her hypothesis, Madanes (1981) cited the example of a bulimic wife whose vomiting was an expression not only of her helplessness, but also of her power. "The symptom was a metaphor for both her submissiveness and rebellion" (Madanes, 1981, p. 40). Therapeutic interventions consisted of paradoxical directives to move the wife into a less submissive position, thereby relieving her of the need to rebel indirectly (i.e., through her symptoms). Once she had learned to be powerful in more appropriate ways, the bulimic wife no longer needed to draw power from the helplessness of her symptoms.

Like Madanes, Boskind-White and White (1983) focused on the bulimic's feelings of helplessness and her conscious desire to be taken care of by her husband. By submitting to the role of the symptomatic wife, however, the bulimic creates marital conflicts that can easily be analyzed in terms of Madanes' balance-of-power theory. In addition, Boskind-White and White noted the undeniable fact that bulimic behaviors, often originally developed as mechanisms for coping with stress, become exaggerated in the marriage when marital conflict increases. In the belief that bulimia is a learned behavior and, therefore, can be unlearned, Boskind-White and White recommended an array of cognitive-behavioral therapeutic techniques, such as rewriting the script, goal contracting, redefining femininity, and behavior rehearsal.

Schwartz, Barrett, and Saba (1985) claimed that a bulimic's marriage tends to mirror both her parents' relationship and her own relationship with her father. This hypothesis suggests that an underlying separation anxiety must be resolved; in fact, as these authors commented, the themes that must be dealt with in marital therapy with a bulimic couple are often the same themes that must be dealt with in their family-of-origin treatment. If the bulimia seems to function in the marriage as it did in the patient's family of origin, it is possible that the bulimia is a continuing expression of the adolescent's struggle for control, autonomy, and independence.

Similarly, Foster (1986) described the relationship between the bulimic patient and her spouse as analogous to the bulimic's relationship with her family of origin in that the bulimic reenacts unresolved conflicts, particularly around separation-individuation issues, within the context of the marital relationship. "In sum, the core dysfunction in eating-disordered couples may be conceptualized as existing on a continuum with respect to separation-individuation" (Foster, 1986, p. 579). Therapeutic interventions with the bulimic couple include disengaging them from their focus on the bulimia and providing them with an opportunity to effect change in other areas of the marital relationship. Specific techniques include

- interrupting hostile interactions and demonstrating their inappropriateness

- teaching alternative methods for coping with stress, such as deep muscle relaxation
- teaching communication and problem-solving skills
- confronting discrepancies between affect and behavior in order to encourage autonomy and directness within the relationship

Once again, it is hypothesized that the adolescent struggle continues and that therapy must attend to the bulimic's need for individuation and independence.

Several hypotheses regarding the bulimic couple emerge from the literature:

1. Bulimia is a metaphor for power, a form of indirect rebellion against an overprotective spouse and/or dominant parent for the submissive individual who cannot rebel more directly.
2. Bulimia functions as a continuation of the adolescent struggle for control, autonomy, and independence in the marriage.
3. Bulimia becomes a way of dealing with stress in the marriage.
4. A bulimic's marriage tends to mirror both her parents' marriage and her relationship with her father.
5. Bulimia may be a way of avoiding feelings of intimacy, particularly sexual intimacy.
6. Bulimia may be an excuse for being "less than perfect" (i.e., unpleasant, irritable, or angry).
7. Bulimia may distract the couple from marital conflict by providing an alternative and ongoing focus.
8. A bulimic may use her condition to get sympathetic and nurturing attention from her spouse.
9. Bulimia may be a desperate cosmetic attempt to control weight in a marriage where thinness is highly valued.

CLINICAL STUDY OF FIVE COUPLES

The hypotheses gleaned from the literature were all explored in the treatment of five bulimic couples. In each case the identified patient is the wife and all five women are in the last stages of recovering from bulimia.

Standardized Interview Schedule

In an unstructured standardized interview, that lasted approximately 2½ hours, the following areas were explored with each couple:

1. demography: occupation; level of education and current salary; proximity to family of origin, both geographical and emotional; number of siblings; length of time married; length of time they had dated each other before marriage; number of children that they already had and the number of children planned
2. eating disorder symptoms: number of years anorexic and/or bulimic; frequency and intensity of binge-purge behavior prior to treatment and now; changes in other eating disorder behavior, such as obsessive thinking about food and weight, excessive exercising, laxative or diuretic abuse, and strenuous dieting or fasting
3. bulimia as a secret: when and how the "secret" was finally revealed, the current roles and rules in keeping the bulimia a secret from others
4. the husbands and fathers of the bulimics: the husband's role in the marriage, the father's role in the family and with the bulimic, similarities and differences in these roles, comparison of the bulimic's marriage to her parents' marriage
5. the function of bulimia in the marriage: whether it was a continuation of the adolescent struggle for control, independence, and autonomy; a way of avoiding feelings, sexual intimacy, and stress; a way of coping with marital conflict; an excuse for being "less than perfect"; a form of indirect rebellion in a struggle for power; a distraction from marital conflict; a way of getting sympathy and attention; an attempt to control weight where thinness is highly valued
6. the effect of treatment (individual, group, or both) and the steps toward recovery on the stability of the marriage

All five couples cooperated during the interview, and each commented independently that the information revealed had increased their level of mutual respect and understanding.

The Study Population

Couple No. 1. John and Judy, aged 34 and 31 respectively, have been married for 3½ years. Judy's bulimia pre-dates the marriage by 2 years, as does a history of alcohol and drug abuse. Although John and Judy lived together for 5 years before they married, John was not aware of her bulimia until 1 year after their marriage.

John, a bright, upwardly mobile attorney, confronted Judy with her bulimia and threatened to divorce her and seek custody of their child if she did not seek help. He had already supported her through her alcohol and drug rehabilitation, and he was running

out of patience. After two consecutive Freedom From Bulimia—
12 Week Group Workshops, in other words, 6 months of group
therapy—and no other therapy—Judy is symptom-free and has
been for almost 1 year. (Freedom From Bulimia—12 Week Group
Workshop^{TM}, is a goal-oriented group workshop for bulimics
offered at Anorexia and Bulimia Resource Center [ABRC] in Coral
Gables, Florida.)

Couple No. 2. Lance and Vicky, aged 26 and 25 respectively,
have been married 2 years, dated 6½ years both during and after
college before they married, have no children yet, but want to
have three or four. Interestingly enough, Vicky's bulimia started in
her third year of college after she and Lance had begun dating.
She claims that "Lance had a lot to do with it; everyone wanted
me to be thin, including him." Lance became aware of Vicky's
bulimia 2 years before the marriage, did not understand it at the
time, and finally dealt with his frustration and feelings of helplessness by encouraging Vicky to seek professional help. After
6 months in the Freedom From Bulimia group workshop, the
frequency of Vicky's bingeing has been reduced from three times
per day to three times per week; the frequency of her purging,
from three times per day to none.

Although bulimia is no longer a problem, overweight and over-
eating are still issues for Vicky, particularly because she knows
that Lance would like her to be thinner. Vicky's frustration with
Lance's expectations, which he often expressed indirectly, motivated them to seek marital therapy. Lance was given an opportunity to express himself more directly, his feelings and opinions
were valued and respected, and the tensions between the couple
were redefined and reduced. Vicky was given permission to relax,
and Lance's expectations were reframed as loving expressions of
concern and caring about her physical and emotional health. Now,
reports Vicky, "when I think about my weight I wonder how I am
going to lose it without bingeing and purging instead of how
quickly I better lose it in order to please Lance."

Couple No. 3. Dawn and Seth, aged 29 and 34 respectively,
have been married 11 years and have 3 children. They dated for
1½ years before they married, and Dawn's bulimia pre-dates their
marriage by 9 years. It was only 3 years ago, i.e., 8 years into the
marriage, that Dawn admitted, during an intensive encounter
experience, to her bulimia. She thought that her admission would

lead her to recovery but she soon found that she could not handle it without therapy.

There is virtually no one in this couple's life who does not know about Dawn's bulimia, particularly because both she and Seth are so proud of her recovery. Before treatment, Dawn's binge-purge activity averaged 3 episodes per day; at this point, she is not purging at all and bingeing on an average of 3 times per week. Dawn was a participant in the Freedom From Bulimia group workshop for 6 months and has continued in individual psychotherapy with me. She is currently working on accepting her body as it is and giving up her obsession with thinness; Seth makes no demands on her in this area and appears to be totally accepting.

Couple No. 4. Jack and Molly, aged 30 and 25 respectively, are college-educated and upwardly mobile, dated for 8 months prior to the marriage, have been married for 1½ years, and have 1 child. Molly's bulimia pre-dates the marriage by 10 years. At its peak, Molly's binge-purge behavior occurred 20 times per day. The frequency of her binge-purge behavior has decreased to three times per week, and her goal is complete recovery. Both she and Jack report that her exercising is no longer compulsive and that her obsessive thinking about her pursuit of thinness and her feelings of being "oversized and unattractive" (the residual distorted thoughts and feelings of a 5′ 5″ tall, very attractive, 110-pound young woman) is much less frequent.

Molly revealed her bulimia to Jack during their courtship as "a thing of the past," although her bulimia was actually rampant at the time. Jack began to suspect that something was wrong, and his suspicions were confirmed after their child was born. In fact, Jack was the one who called to inquire about the services of the ABRC; and shortly after his call, Molly came in for her interview. She was a member of the Freedom From Bulimia group workshop for 6 months and has also received individual psychotherapy and limited marital therapy. Both Jack and Molly are now comfortable in telling others about Molly's bulimia, and both report feeling proud that her recovery has been so remarkable.

Couple No. 5. Gloria and Josh, aged 35 and 32 respectively, dated for 1½ years before they married and have been married 3 years. They have no children; while Josh is certain that he would like a family, Gloria is presently undecided. Gloria's eating disorder pre-dates the marriage by 13 years. At the height of her bulimia, she was bingeing and purging 40 times per day. Therapy has reduced the frequency of her binge-purge activity dramatically to 1 or 2 times per day, and her goal is complete recovery. Josh remembers very clearly how and when he first found out about Gloria's bulimia: "We were driving in the car and the radio was on, announcing the death of Karen Carpenter . . . later that evening, under the influence of alcohol, Gloria told me, 'I have what Karen Carpenter had . . . it's serious.'" At that point, Gloria was bingeing and purging 40 times a day, and Josh was absolutely unaware of the problem.

Another year passed, during which Gloria's father died and Josh and Gloria married. Despite Josh's quiet encouragement, Gloria resisted treatment until one day Josh arranged an interview for Gloria at the ABRC. Gloria participated in the Freedom From Bulimia group workshop for 6 months. For the first eight sessions, until she began to trust the group, Josh drove her to each session. Gloria continues to make progress, and Josh continues to encourage her quietly.

Themes and Concepts That Emerged in Treatment

Several themes emerged from the interviews with these five couples. In all but one case, the husband clearly encouraged, insisted, or actually sought professional treatment for his wife.

Secrecy. While secrecy was a major issue for the bulimic herself, the bulimia never became a shared secret between the husband and wife; rather, the disclosure or detection of the condition created an opportunity for the husband to encourage or insist that the wife seek professional help.

The reasons that the women never voluntarily admitted to their bulimia were pointedly clear and painfully stated. Molly recalled that "I kept bulimia a secret from Jack for the same reasons I kept it from everybody else . . . because I was guilty and full of shame, and if anyone knew, I might be forced to give it up." Vicky recalled that "I began to feel the bulimia was becoming unmanageable . . . I was becoming 'desperate' . . . but I remember thinking, if I tell him, then I have to get better." It appears that as "disgusting" a secret as the bulimia had become, the humiliation of disclosure was believed to be far worse than the pain of secrecy.

All bulimics feel some ambivalence about giving up their symptoms. Because of the universal self-soothing, self-nurturing function of bulimia, as well as its function as a weight control measure, all bulimics are consciously or unconsciously deeply fearful of losing their binge-purge behavior. Learning to express feelings, to regulate themselves in other ways, and to deal with the sometimes rational (more often irrational) fear of weight gain are the most necessary and frustrating therapeutic tasks on the bulimic's road to recovery. In the mind of the secretive bulimic, to confess her bulimia to her spouse and to commit to professional help is fraught with more risks and more fear of the unknown than is the bulimia itself. Therefore, the bulimic unconsciously continues to choose what is already known and what she has persuaded herself is "safe."

Other fears that the women expressed in the interviews were the fear of losing the relationship if the husband were to find out about the bulimia or, more likely and realistically, the fear of losing his approval. The fear of disapproval was expressed almost identically by Dawn and Vicky: "I feared what my husband would think of me if he knew about my disgusting habits." That most of the women in this study were continuing their adolescent search for independence has been confirmed. That they were still struggling to win their husband's approval further explains their reluctance to confess—the fear of husband's/father's explicit disapproval of the bulimia and the need for at least implicit approval of body shape and size.

Although none of the women consciously felt that the bulimia had helped them gain or exert control in the marriage, some of them felt that their husbands had lost trust in them, at least temporarily, because of the way in which the secret was exposed. Molly stated that "since I lied so frequently to cover bulimic episodes, and I often couldn't get out of my own problems to focus on his, I suppose he lost trust in me." Vicky reported that trust was indeed shaken: "In general, he felt if I could keep this big a lie, what else could I lie about?" The husbands all agreed that they were not prepared to act as "detectives" or "policemen" during their wives' recovery, that they could understand the reasons for the secrecy, and that they were working on regaining trust and preventing mistrust from entering other areas of the marriage.

Similarities between Husbands and Fathers. Data on the hypothesis that bulimics' husbands tend to be similar to their fathers were inconclusive at best. Three of the five women described their husbands as more dissimilar than similar to their fathers; interestingly, all three reported the same differences, describing their fathers as much less emotionally involved, more passive, and more detached than their husbands. Vicky specifically described Lance as much more like her mother. While she felt her father's love was always unconditional, she said she had a similar fear of disappointing either Lance or her mother. She added that they had a similar knack for being indirect and delivering mixed messages; for example, both Lance and Vicky's mother continue to deliver the double message, "Be thin and eat and enjoy life with me." Finally, Judy reported unequivocally that "I feel like I married my father

. . . he reads constantly like my father, doesn't talk about feelings like my father, distances himself from me like my father," and so forth. In four cases, the descriptions of the fathers were strikingly similar.

Rejected Hypotheses. Of the nine hypotheses that emerged from the literature, three of them were unanimously rejected by the couples in the study group. No one felt that the bulimia was ever offered as an excuse for being "less than perfect," and no one believed that the bulimia served the wife positively as a way to elicit sympathy and attention. Furthermore, all were somewhat proud that their marriages differed significantly from those of their families of origin and expressed the perceived differences in a way that implied a healthier level of functioning. For example, Jack and Molly agreed that "we communicate a lot more directly. It may be more painful, but it's direct. My parents' communication was always 'second level'." Vicky described her parents' marriage as one in which "Mom was dominant, and Dad went along," while "Lance and I struggle for equality. If anything, our roles are reversed. If one of us is dominant, it's Lance at the moment, and I'm the one who tends to go along." Seth and Dawn agreed that "we are more open with our feelings than Dawn's parents were; we are very social, always going out with other couples. In fact, we are totally different and live totally different lives."

In the "family systems" view of bulimia, the marital relationship is perceived as a system that maintains the bulimic's symptoms. Theoretically, "the bulimic marries . . . a person who makes it possible for her to continue her relationship with food and, therefore, with bulimia" (Barrett & Schwartz, 1987, p. 25). Furthermore, the bulimic chooses someone who not only permits, but also "needs the bulimia and the associated behaviors (e.g., dependency, lack of intimacy)" (Barrett & Schwartz, 1987 p. 25). These theoretical assumptions stem from the traditional view of the alcoholic couple in which the non-alcoholic partner is seen as a "co-alcoholic" or an "enabler," an individual who "needs" the alcoholic partner as much as the alcoholic partner needs the symptoms of alcoholism. The co-addiction or complementarity model has not yet been established for bulimic couples as it has for alcoholic couples, however. Furthermore, the data in this study do not validate such a hypothesis.

In none of these cases was there any evidence that the husband was receiving any "payoff" from his wife's symptomatology, nor was there any evidence of an effort to sabotage recovery. In all cases, follow-up showed that the marriages had grown stronger and more optimistic. One can speculate that perhaps the secret was "known" on an unconscious level or that needs (e.g., for power, dependency, lack of intimacy) were somehow being met on an unconscious level, but it is difficult to support such a speculation without any evidence of sabotage or marital breakdown. The husbands in this study appeared to be much more supportive of the treatment than of the illness; they all reported feeling relief once professional treatment had begun. Moreover, their pride and continued concern were evident throughout the various stages of recovery.

Partially Confirmed Hypotheses. Some hypotheses received "mixed reviews." While most of the couples agreed that bulimia did not function as a way to avoid sexual intimacy, the pendulum of responses swung from that of Jack and Molly who were outraged at the suggestion, "Sexual intimacy? Never!" to that of Lance and Vicky who quickly agreed that Vicky's frequent statements, "Don't touch me . . . I feel gross," were definitely a sexual turnoff. In addition, because of Vicky's overweight and their mutual strong desire for her to become thinner, they agreed that desire, frequency, and pleasure were all negatively affected by Vicky's poor body image.

The hypothesis that bulimia functions to provide an ongoing focus in the marriage and, therefore, a distraction from other marital conflicts met with some interesting responses. Most couples denied that the bulimia ever took center stage, claiming that communication was always open in other areas. Despite the husband's eagerness for the wife to enter treatment, once treatment began, they agreed that recovery was really *her* responsibility. Jack and Molly, however, reported that *her* bulimia and *his* interest in it did "create a real strong bond between us" and that, at times, "our energies were all used up just dealing with it." Because his insistence that she get help coincided with the birth of their child, both now feel that the bulimia overshadowed other issues that "other young couples would undoubtedly be dealing with during their first pregnancy." Now that Molly is in an advanced recovery stage, they find themselves dealing with issues that they knew existed, but ignored, earlier in their marriage.

All couples but one agreed that bulimia was not a cosmetic attempt to control weight. Only Lance and Vicky, the same couple who felt that bulimia served to avoid sexual intimacy, felt that there was a cosmetic factor to Vicky's bulimia. They agreed that Lance had a great deal to do with maintaining Vicky's bulimia in that he consistently admitted to his preference for thin women. "The only way I could please him," reported Vicky, was "to continue my purging so I wouldn't gain too much weight." Lance and Vicky elected to have marital therapy during Vicky's group therapy, and the marital therapy appeared to make a substantial contribution to the recovery. Lance needed help in modifying his attitudes and behavior toward Vicky and in becoming more open in the positive expression of the feelings that he has always had for her. At the moment, Vicky is the only one of the five former bulimics who is overweight, a battle she has fought since childhood; this opens up the whole question of set-point theory, self-acceptance, and the injustice of societal and cultural expectations, particularly for women who have an obvious hereditary component to their weight problem.

The "fear of fat" that often triggers and then continues to fuel the bulimic experience may have its origins in the bulimic's early family history, possibly as far back as the parents' response to the child's body during infancy. Negative body image and body image disturbances have also been linked to the mother-daughter relationship and the mother's transmission of body image to her daughter (Kearney-Cooke, 1986). When the bulimia takes on "a life of its own," it serves as a continuous reminder and reinforcement of the bulimic's negative body image. The majority of bulimics report wanting to be 5 to 10 pounds lighter; those few who are satisfied with their body weight "hate" some part of their body shape, usually the abdomen, thighs, or hips. This negative body image remains at the core of the bulimic's cognitive system; as the self is constantly devalued, self-esteem sinks lower and lower. Depression can be seen as both a byproduct and an end-product of this vicious cycle.

Body image distortions must be corrected if the treatment of bulimia is to be successful. Therefore, opportunities must be provided to help the bulimic create a more positive body image,

> one where the body is no longer used as a vehicle of expression for repressed feelings and a "battle-ground" for acting out these feelings, that instead is accepted as a positive source of feelings, physical needs, and information about oneself. (Kearney-Cooke, 1986, p. 2)

Confirmed Hypotheses. All the women basically agreed that the more conflict in the marriage, the more overwhelmed and out of control they felt. "I go straight to the refrigerator . . . you always go back to what you know." Boskind-White and White (1983) were the first to comment on the undeniable and ironic fact that, while the familiarity of bulimia often makes it a mechanism for coping with stress, it is likely to become exaggerated when marital conflict increases. This finding certainly lends credibility to the belief, based on learning theory, that bulimia is a learned behavioral response to either external or internal anxiety and, therefore, treatment must include an array of cognitive-behavioral techniques based on the reciprocal belief that learned behavior can be unlearned.

The struggle for power and the continued search for adolescent autonomy were found to be interrelated. What began for Judy in her adolescence as a drug and alcohol problem developed into bulimia after her appetite for drugs and alcohol was curbed. She sees all three disorders as "self-destructive behavior, all designed so I wouldn't have to deal with my feelings; I hated myself so much; I felt so out of control." These comments resemble the universal feelings of many adolescents who are struggling to separate and define themselves, feeling lost and hating their own dependence, unconsciously choosing rebellious behaviors in order to act out their confusion. Judy still did not know who she was when she entered her marriage; "I still felt like a little girl, needing to be taken care of."

The interaction between the metaphor for power hypothesis and the struggle for independence is clear in Judy's case. Her bulimia rendered her submissive which, by definition, gave her a position in the marriage, albeit an inferior one. Until she recovered from the bulimia, she felt that she did not deserve to be "an equal partner in the marriage," because she "wasn't finished growing up." Now that she has recovered, she is asserting herself within the marriage, is reaching out to her parents in order to redefine her role as their daughter, and is hoping to have a second child in the near future.

Lance and Vicky both agree that Vicky's bulimia was her way of saying to Lance (i.e., "the domineering one"), "Leave me alone—let me be who I am." This struggle for power, independence, and separateness began in Vicky's adolescence; it was interrupted by the premature death of her father, to whom she was overattached. Vicky is still struggling with her own autonomy. Interestingly enough, it is Vicky who feels that her husband is much more like her mother than her father. With therapy, the balance of power in the marriage has definitely changed, and this couple probably have more true equality than any of the others.

In the case of Molly and Jack, once again the power and the autonomy themes interact. Molly admits "I should be able to listen to my own thoughts, yet I still call on people for guidance. I'm afraid to be alone with myself and my own thoughts. Bulimia was my way of being defiant and then turning the guilt on myself." Molly is now aware that her bulimia was an act of rebellion leading to a false sense of self, that her independence from her family of origin is far from complete, and that what she really wants is "to be free." Because she has not, until recently, felt the emotional freedom to express her own autonomy, the bulimia became a unique metaphor for power in her marriage.

Molly reports, "If I've been too strong, overstepped my bounds, then I feel I revert to bulimia in order to recalibrate . . . if I really overdid it, really spoke out, I feel myself beginning to shake all over . . . then I binge and purge and then I don't feel so strong about being so strong . . . I don't want to make waves and bingeing and purging to me is not making waves . . . it's passive, submissive."

Jack commented that he had observed Molly repeat this cycle many times despite his attempts to compliment her on her strength. Despite Jack's genuine acceptance of her strength, Molly continued for some time to "dislike the strong, domineering, overbearing self" that she felt she was becoming. "What if I hurt someone . . . I remind myself I'm not so strong and even provide my own self-punishment." She continues to binge and purge occasionally in order to "reduce stress and feel better."

TREATING THE "BULIMIC COUPLE"

Based on the study findings, the goals of marital therapy with "bulimic" couples include

- redistributing the balance of power in the marriage
- helping the bulimic to disengage from her unhealthy relationships with her family of origin and differentiate between adolescent dependency and adult interdependence
- providing the couple with an expanded repertoire of skills for self-expression and alternative methods for coping with stress

Used selectively and in varying combinations, depending on the degree of marital dysfunction, interpersonal strengths, and level of therapeutic involvement, the following techniques should be considered in efforts to achieve these goals:

1. Strategic techniques, such as the paradoxical directive to replace the binge-purge behavior with the behavior that the bulimia may be suppressing, such as an expression of anger or self-assertion.
2. Other strategic techniques, such as relabeling or "positive connotation" (Selvini-Palazzoli, Cecchin, Prata, & Boscolo, 1978). For example, the therapist may say to the wife about her detached husband, "Your husband is not ignoring you . . . in fact, he is actually freeing you up to recover at your own pace, in your own way, because he knows you are very strong," and to the husband about his bulimic spouse, "Your wife is actually risking intimacy and disclosure in the marriage, knowing it might cost her the marriage, but trusting you to understand and be patient."
3. Multigenerational family therapy, in order to work through family-of-origin conflicts (Boszormenyi-Nagy & Framo, 1965).
4. Assertiveness training for the couple, in order that they both learn to express feelings, thoughts, and opinions in a manner that is direct, honest, and appropriate without violating the rights of the other (Lange & Jakubowski, 1976).
5. Communication training, including didactic instructions, behavior rehearsal, practice by the couple, and feedback from the therapist (Jacobson & Anderson, 1980). Particularly important is the teaching of listening and expressive skills (Guerney, 1977) so that both partners will feel understood, free to engage in affective expression, and more willing to

risk self-disclosure. It is also vital to ensure that each partner knows how to ask for a desired behavior change in the other.

6. Conflict resolution skills, essential for the couple to remain interdependent rather than family-dependent. Problem-solving training modeled, practiced, and learned in two phases, the definition phase and the resolution phase, is extremely helpful in reducing marital stress (Jacobson & Margolin, 1979).

7. Deep muscle relaxation and/or self-hypnosis with guided imagery, as alternative methods of handling stress.

8. Movement therapy or body image treatment in order to help the patient understand the underlying meanings of fat and thin, and to develop a less distorted, more positive body image (Kearney-Cooke, 1986).

9. Cognitive restructuring with a liberal sprinkling of rational emotive therapy (Ellis & Harper, 1961) in order to reduce the stress of unrealistic expectations of self and others.

Continued research is necessary to determine just how functional bulimia really is in a marital system before marital therapy can unequivocally be recommended for every bulimic who is also married. Research must also address the question of the relative benefits of individual, group, and marital therapy for the married eating-disordered patient. Although it is hoped that the doors opened by these five married couples have shed some light on the bulimic couple, many more doors must be opened both statistically and clinically in order to prove that marital therapy is effective for the bulimic couple.

REFERENCES

American Psychiatric Association. (1980). *Diagnostic and statistical manual of mental disorders: III.* Washington, DC: Author.

Barrett, M.J., & Schwartz, R. (1987). Couples therapy for bulimia. In J.E. Harkaway (Ed.), *The family therapy collections: Eating Disorders* (vol. 20). Rockville, MD: Aspen Publishers, *20,* pp. 25–39.

Boskind-White, M., & White, W.C. (1983). *Bulimarexia: The binge/purge cycle.* New York: W.W. Norton.

Boszormenyi-Nagy, I., & Framo, J. (Eds.). (1965). *Intensive family therapy: Theoretical and practical aspects.* New York: Harper & Row.

Bruch, H. (1973). *Eating disorders: Obesity, anorexia nervosa and the person within.* New York: Basic Books.

Casper, R. (1983). On the emergence of bulimia nervosa as a syndrome. *International Journal of Eating Disorders, 2,* 3–16.

Ellis, A., & Harper, R. (1961). *A new guide to rational living.* North Hollywood, CA: Wilshire Book Co.

Foster, S. (1986). Marital treatment of eating disorders. In N. Jacobson & A. Gurman (Eds.), *Clinical handbook of marital therapy* (pp. 575–592). New York: Guilford Press.

Garfinkel, P.E., & Garner, D.M. (1982). *Anorexia nervosa: A multi-dimensional perspective.* New York: Brunner/Mazel.

Guerney, B. (1977). *Relationship enhancement.* San Francisco: Jossey-Bass.

Halmi, K.A., Falk, J.R., & Schwartz, E. (1981). Binge eating and vomiting: A survey of a college population. *Psychological Medicine, 11,* 607–706.

Jacobson, N.S., & Anderson, E.A. (1980). The effects of behavioral rehearsal and feed-back on the acquisition of problem solving skills in distressed and non-distressed couples. *Behavioral Research and Therapy, 18,* 25–36.

Jacobson, N.A., & Margolin, G. (1979). *Marital therapy: Strategies based on social learning and behavior exchange principles.* New York: Brunner/Mazel.

Kearney-Cooke, A. (1986). *Feminist approaches to body image disturbances among women with eating disorders.* Paper presented at the American Psychological Association Pre-Convention Workshop on the Psychology of Women, Washington, D.C.

Lange, A.J., & Jakubowski, P. (1976). *Responsible assertive behavior.* Champaign, IL: Research Press.

Madanes, C. (1981). *Strategic family therapy.* San Francisco: Jossey-Bass.

Pyle, R.L., Mitchell, J.E., & Eckert, E.D. (1981). Bulimia: A report of thirty four cases. *Journal of Clinical Psychiatry, 42,* 60–64.

Schwartz, R.C., Barrett, M.I., & Saba, G. (1985). Family therapy for bulimia. In D. Garner & P. Garfinkel (Eds.), *Handbook of psychotherapy for anorexia nervosa and bulimia.* New York: Guilford Press.

Selvini-Palazzoli, M., Cecchin, G., Prata, G., & Boscolo, L. (1978). *Paradox and counter paradox: A new model in the therapy of the family in schizophrenic transaction.* New York: Jason-Aronson.

7. Treating the Gay Couple within the Context of Their Families of Origin

David Keller, PsyD
Institute for Comprehensive Family Therapy
Spring House, Pennsylvania

Hugh Rosen, DSW
Professor
Hahneman University
Philadelphia, Pennsylvania

If a man does not keep pace with his companions, perhaps it is because he hears a different drummer. Let him step to the music which he hears, however measured or far away. (Thoreau, 1966, p. 215)

In spite of the U.S. Supreme Court decision of June 30, 1986, which questions sexuality between two men, male couples are continuing to seek therapy, and therapists are beginning to focus on their treatment (Brown & Zimmer, 1986; Forstein, 1986; Moses & Hawkins, 1978). As Maslow (1962) noted, the need to belong is a more basic and instinctual need within the species than is self-esteem or self-actualization. Gay men are beginning to listen to their feelings and their minds, rather than to societal dictates, and are more openly expressing the desire and need for a primary, intimate relationship. Effective, competent treatment of the gay male couple requires both an efficacious treatment plan and a sensitivity to issues that are idiosyncratic and particular to a gay male couple.

Although there are many more similarities than differences between homo-sexual and heterosexual relationships, gay men must confront some issues within their lives that heterosexual individuals do not experience. The way in which gay men deal with these issues is the difference between their toleration of their existence and their true acceptance of themselves and creation of a healthy, loving, growing relationship.

VALUES OF GAY COUPLES

. Based on self-report questionnaires, Bell and Weinberg (1978) noted that, like heterosexual persons, homosexuals want an ongoing love relationship— not a series of casual, short-term relationships. Love, commitment, and companionship, as well as sex, appear to be valued components in a gay relationship (Peplau, 1982), just as they are in a heterosexual relationship. A study of mostly white, educated gay men who currently or previously had a "romantic/sexual" relationship with a man indicated that gay men place great importance on intimacy, defined as being able to talk about their most intimate feelings; on mutually independent careers so that both persons are financially and occupationally/professionally independent; and on sexual compatibility, attraction, and interest (Peplau & Cochran, 1981). Additionally, gay men believe that each person within the relationship should have an independent group of friends from whom to derive social and emotional support apart from the lover/partner. These men have a stated preference for equal power relationships, although research indicates that age difference actually determines the expected dominance patterns and the decision-making protocol within a gay relationship (Harry, 1982).

ROLE PLAYING AND ROLE MODELS

Because the heterosexual model is the most visible one and the one in which most persons were reared, many individuals adhere to the myth that one gay male lover assumes the role of wife, while the other assumes the role of husband. Although some gay male couples may mirror stereotypical heterosexual relationships, doing so does not meet the needs of most gay male couples (Peplau, 1982). In fact, some research data show that satisfaction within any relationship, whether homosexual or heterosexual, is inversely proportional to adherence to rigid, stereotypical male-female roles in those relationships (Maracek, Finn, & Cardell, 1982). Although it could be expected that male-identified and female-identified gays would naturally assume a clear-cut division of roles, this does not appear to be the case (McWhirter & Mattison, 1982).

Only recently have gay men begun to consider the legitimacy of their relationships. After being reared within the heterosexual model, two men have few role models for coming together and learning not only how to work out the practical details of day-to-day living, but also how to meet each other's emotional needs and potentiate each other's lives. From a clinical perspective, it appears more therapeutically useful to determine each partner's emotional needs and strengths (e.g., discipline, nurturing, and programming for success and confidence) without the labels of gender identity. Whether because of biological or socialization factors, it may be true that men and women contribute somewhat different strengths to a heterosexual relationship. The use of gender labels is operationally nonspecific, however. In some cases, it may even be diminutive, because it places a differential value on gender and limits the resources that each person brings to a relationship.

HOMOPHOBIA AND ITS EFFECTS

> The single most important factor about homosexuality as it exists in this culture is the perceived hostility of the societal reactions that surround it. (Plummer, 1975, p. 102)

It is extremely traumatic to be gay in the face of a rejecting, hostile society. A gay man is forced to live without the supports and sanctions that society usually offers to others. For example, maintaining a religious belief becomes an issue for gay men, because most religions condemn homosexuality. Although alternative gay religious organizations have been developed, a nagging sense of rejection and the lack of complete acceptance reinforce the perception of the illegitimacy of the gay experience.

Acceptance of a gay child is one of the most difficult and potentially divisive issues that a family must face. Parents must cope with the disappointment caused by their child's deviation from prescribed rules and the probability that this child will not give them grandchildren. They must face their feelings of inadequacy and failure as parents. The father perceives a threat to his own manhood in having a gay son. Falling victim to societal pressure, fathers usually feel shame and embarrassment. The gay son must cope with the knowledge that he is a disappointment to his parents and a sense that he is never quite as acceptable as his heterosexual siblings. Because intimacy includes being and feeling accepted, bridging this gap becomes a lifetime endeavor that at times seems impossible for both the family and the gay son. Outside the nuclear family, a gay man must deal with the possible rejection of grandparents, aunts, uncles, cousins, and the family at large. In the absence of prescribed rules, parents and families of gay men must find their own way to a satisfying relationship.

Homosexuality also becomes a potentially divisive issue with friends. Women friends may be disappointed to discover that a man is gay because he is no longer a potential sexual partner, and men friends may fear that they will be accused of homosexuality by association. Thus, a gay man finds his social circle of "straight" friends in flux, with some supportive and others anxious to sever all ties when they become aware that he is gay. As a result, although a gay man indeed values his heterosexual relationships, he usually discovers that he also needs a group of gay friends, who become his "gay family." In this group, acceptance of his gayness is not an issue; he can share common experiences and values; and there are mentors who can teach him how to make his life work.

Discrimination may become an issue at the workplace, in school, and in society at large. Professional and occupational advancements may be affected. Young people in school are especially cruel during the years of budding sexual development, teasing and taunting anyone who is different. Society at large provides support for heterosexual couples, but not for same sex couples. Billboards and magazines herald the joys of Jim and Susan, not those of Bob and Steve. Gay jokes abound. Indeed, violence toward both gays and lesbians is rampant so that they must not only weather social rejection, but also at times be on guard for their life.

Gay men do not go unscathed by any of these outside forces; rather, they are profoundly affected by these forces. The societal ban against same sex relationships and harsh judgment of those who are gay suggest that the gay person is not as "good" a person as others. A gay man learns that many of the rewards in life, such as unlimited occupational opportunities, fair housing, equal and fair judicial treatment, and general respect from society, may not be within his purview. Although the American Psychiatric Association (1980) no longer lists homosexuality as a mental illness in the *Diagnostic and Statistical Manual of Mental Disorders,* a gay man may not even receive deep acceptance as a person within the therapeutic context; some professionals have attitudes and values that may lead them to undertake subtle attempts to change the sexual orientation of the client. As with all persons, these reactions and values are internalized and to varying degrees, influence a gay person's life.

Just as people carry into their relationships the attitudes and values of their nuclear family, they also bear the baggage of societal reactions. As clinicians have observed, the child who is scapegoated within the family may truly believe that he is inferior and may become a victim within his primary relationship. Similarly, the gay person may internalize societal reactions to his gayness as self-hatred, which has profound effects on both the gay man and his relationships (Maylon, 1982; Stein & Cohen, 1984). Several fundamental beliefs developed by gay men impede the development of their relationships:

1. Being gay is inferior; therefore, gay relationships are inferior and only mimic the real thing.
2. Gay relationships do not and should not work.
3. Gay relationships are not and should not be enduring.

The basic belief of most gay men, as well as of many professionals, is that a good and enduring, emotionally satisfying relationship between two gay men is impossible. Furthermore, most support systems in his environment reinforce this belief. Because it decreases the motivation for bonding with another man, as well as for developing a stable, ongoing unit, this belief is devastating to the process of developing a primary gay relationship. Internalized homophobia defined as self-hatred in gay men diminishes their self-respect and, in turn, their respect for another man. It increases their self-doubts and self-rejection and, in turn, their rejection of others. If two men succeed in working through internal issues, bonding and developing a relationship, they only invite more negative societal reaction. A single man can pass as a heterosexual, but a gay couple cannot. In addition, the family support that enhances the joy of a heterosexual relationship and helps to maintain the bond in difficult times is often withheld from a gay couple. Those who have worked through these issues with their families to the point of receiving genuine, quality support are few in number. Our professional belief is that people have a richer experience of themselves when in relationships with others and that a deeper level of intimacy is enhanced and enriched in primary relationships, heterosexual or homosexual, which in turn enrich society in general.

AIDS AND ITS IMPACT

Acquired immune deficiency syndrome (AIDS) is currently having a strong impact on the gay community (Morin, Charles, & Maylon, 1984; Nichols & Strow, 1984). In addition to caring for their sick and burying their dead, gay men are dealing with a reactionary backlash and, in some cases, increased discrimination. Many are experiencing a great deal of guilt, as this disease has been dubbed "the gay disease." Only time will reveal the precise effects of AIDS on gay relationships, but already there are more monogamous relationships and fewer open relationships. The intense fear and panic among gays has decreased the emphasis on sex and increased that on "relating."

Certainly, relationships in which one person has AIDS are in a state of fear, grief, and havoc. At a relatively young age, many couples are suddenly having to deal with the financial and emotional devastation of death. They are being shunned by previous friends who are fearful, which produces a crisis within their support system. With its political and social implications, as well as the resultant emotional drain on persons with AIDS, their lovers, and the gay community at large, AIDS has contributed to a tremendous setback for gay men in their effort to gain further human rights.

A burden falls on the clinician to deal with such AIDS-related issues as fear of contraction of AIDS, the administration of AIDS antibody tests to gay men, and the use of sexually safe practices to prevent the exchange of body fluids.

GAY FATHERS

As gay men are beginning to accept themselves and their homosexuality more fully, gay fathers are becoming a clinical entity. Despite separation and/or divorce, it is important for fathers—gay or straight—to maintain a parental relationship with their biological children. All too often, however, guilt over separation from his wife and guilt over his homosexuality cause a gay man to leave his children not only physically, but also psychologically, when he leaves the marriage.

In therapy with the family of origin, discussions of parenting foster the gay person's individuation, which promotes differentiation from past negative and positive introjects (Bowen, 1978) and enhances the quality of love relationships. Additionally, it promotes honesty and self-disclosure, producing a more integrated individual. Improving the gay person's relationships with his children fosters greater personal growth for the father, alleviates guilt for being gay and separating from the spouse, and maintains object relations that lead to a better integrated adult gay man. Successful parenting is a precursor to a healthy adult relationship for both the parent and the child.

Therapists may become overly focused on treating symptoms without considering the context of the person's life. Gay fathers who seek therapy for such problems as anxiety, depression, or difficulties with lovers need to be dealt with in the full context of their lives, including relationships with their children, their lover, their family of origin, and themselves. Shifting flexibly between all these levels, therapy should lead to an enrichment of every major aspect of the client's life (Keller, 1986).

THERAPEUTIC MODEL

As more and more gay men decide to take on a life partner, their needs and demands as a couple are receiving more attention in the literature on therapy and counseling (McWhirter & Mattison, 1984; Reece, 1979; Silverstein, 1981). Because people are more similar than they are different, family therapy has much to offer a gay couple. Many approaches to therapy have been explored and many theories developed, including psychodynamic, behavioral, and systemic theories. In recent years, however, attempts have been made to integrate and synthesize family therapy theories (Kaslow, 1981).

The Kirschners (1986) have synthesized psychodynamic, behavioral, and systemic theories into one coherent approach—comprehensive family therapy (CFT). A dialectical metatheory, CFT includes the interaction between the changing person and the changing environment, the family, and the process of change itself. This process is described within the context of the family holon, which is composed of the intrapsychic phenomena of individual family members and the systemic transactions of the family members.

Within the family holon, movement or change in any family member affects all family members and the family as a whole. The clinician not only attempts to ameliorate dysfunction, but also actively accelerates the process and elevates the family to its potential functional levels. According to CFT, the form of the family holon includes the behavioral transactions between the family member and the intrapsychic phenomena of each member.

Behavioral Transactions

The therapist who uses CFT conceptualizes behavioral transactions as three interlocking and interrelated subsystems: (1) the marital transaction, (2) the rearing transaction, and (3) the independent transactions. The marital transaction, the central hub of the family, consists of the patterns of behavioral interaction between the couple. This relationship is shaped by the individuals, and the individuals are shaped intrapsychically by the relationship and by the other partner. The rearing transaction includes all the transactions between parents and children, between parents regarding the children, and among the siblings. It encompasses all provisions for growth (e.g., nurturing, discipline, and programming), as well as patterns of dysfunction (e.g., enmeshment, distantiation, and conflict). The rearing transaction is governed and limited by the quality of the marital transaction. Independent transactions involve each family member's interaction with the outside world, for example, at work, in school, and through religious and social activities.

Intrapsychic Phenomena: The Self System

Central within the family are the intrapsychic phenomena (referred to as the self systems) of the spouses, which developed during transactions in the family of origin. The self systems shape the marital, rearing, and independent transactions. The parents project and assign roles for the children, programming them to fit within their own intrapsychic needs. The self system is composed of three levels: (1) the foundation of the ego, (2) sexual identification, and (3) triangulation.

The foundation of the ego is at the core of the self system. It develops in the child's basic early relationship with the mother, resulting in internalization of the mothering person and, it is hoped, a feeling of belongingness and lovableness. After sufficient mothering, a child can individuate and develop a sense of separate self (Mahler, 1980).

With CFT, it is considered better and more congruent for individuals to feel like a person of their biological gender. Homoaffiliative needs, or the need to be with the parent of the same sex, govern and teach a child how to be and feel good as a man or a woman. Because the child identifies with both parents to varying degrees, the therapist examines the qualities of both masculine and feminine identifications in order to determine their effect within the primary relationship.

As a child begins to develop a sense of self, a relationship develops between the child and the mothering person. Eventually, the child forms a relationship with both parents, and a group develops. Within this triangular relationship, the child must deal with competitive struggles for attention, loyalty, and alliance. At this Oedipal level, the child begins to develop the patterns that will determine how he or she relates to a lover.

PATHOLOGY

Each member of a couple has chosen a partner to help reinstate the original symbiosis in his or her family of origin. This symbiotic state may include such pathology as fear of intimacy, which triggers basic fears that, in turn, reinforce the fear of intimacy with another person—namely, the partner or lover. Using the CFT approach, the therapist considers the degree and intensity of the basic fears at the foundation of the ego (e.g., annihilation, abandonment, and engulfment). As core anxieties in all persons, these fears shape the self system and ultimately determine the quality of primary relationships. The intensity of the basic fears is directly proportional to the degree that primary needs were met during the rearing years by the mothering one. To the degree that these needs were not met, pathology is present. The goal of the CFT clinician is to remediate the immediate problem and to elevate the family holon to a level of optimum functioning, using a reparenting approach that allows access to the regressive, inner world of each person.

OPTIMAL FAMILY PROCESS

If the family is a holon in the process of transformation, the CFT clinician vigorously works toward an end state, or telos, for both the family and its individual members. Through the model of optimal functioning, therapy actively moves clients and families toward that telos in order to determine their true potential based on the therapist's evaluation of their potential for growth. As each person in a family or couple learns new skills and attains new levels of competence, he or she re-experiences old fears (e.g., feelings of inadequacy or inferiority). As this natural regression ensues, healing inputs are provided first by the therapist and later by the partner as the client returns to the love object for reassurance and nurturing. The entire process is referred to as progressive abreactive reaction (Stein, 1980).

Each partner or lover takes responsibility not only for his own growth, but also for that of the other partner when appropriate, thus enhancing the growth potential of both. The process of dedicating themselves to the growth of the other leads them to transcend the self, and selfishness comes to mean a win-win situation. This process deepens the relationship, because each becomes an important and integral part of the other's growth; thus, intimacy is magnified. Each partner within the marriage or couple serves as a reparental figure to the other, repairing old wounds from the family of origin and elevating each other and the relationship to new functional levels of competence and satisfaction.

CASE EXAMPLE

One of the authors (D.K.) saw the following couple in therapy. Kevin, a gay man in his mid-40s, called for a consultation about himself and his lover, Steve, also in his mid-40s. Although the couple had lived together for 9 years, Steve was currently having an affair with one of his employees, a 22-year-old man. Kevin stated that Steve was definitely not interested in dissolving their relationship, but wanted the freedom to develop outside relationships. The couple had not engaged in sexual activity within their relationship for the past year, an arrangement that was entirely unacceptable to Kevin. He was considering terminating the relationship unless change occurred quickly. When the therapist inquired about working with both men together, Kevin stated that Steve had adamantly refused to seek outside intervention.

Because the therapist felt that immediate intervention was needed, and because Kevin was apparently motivated to work on the relationship, the therapist suggested that Kevin confront Steve and threaten to terminate the relationship unless the affair was promptly ended. Two days later, Steve called for an appointment.

Steve was a depressed, dependent person who appeared to be sitting on much anger. He had obtained his bachelor's degree and was an entry level interviewer in a personnel department for a major business firm. He had been in this position for 5 years, was not progressing, and was very unhappy with his employment. Steve had been divorced for 3 years and had seen his 8-year-old son only occasionally since that time. He had no outside interests and no friends. His activities consisted of reading and watching TV. When the therapist explored his relationship with Kevin, Steve stated that he did not want to terminate the relationship; however, he did not find the current relationship fulfilling, and he was unhappy with his life in general. Although he felt hopeless and helpless, he agreed to enter couples therapy with Kevin.

Kevin was a successful department chairman at a major university, who seemed very anxious and tense. He worked hard and had few outside interests; he had many acquaintances, but no real friends. He was very driven, somewhat critical, and alcoholic, although his drinking did not interfere with his professional career. Although he had not developed any emotionally significant affairs during his 9 years with Steve, he had engaged in casual sex with other men and had encouraged Steve to do the same.

At the next conjoint session, Steve stated that, initially, he had been attracted to Kevin's aggressiveness; Kevin stated that he had been attracted to Steve's warmth and sensitivity. The therapist discovered that a typical homeostatic sequence occurred between the two. Kevin pursued more closeness, and Steve attempted to please him. Kevin then became critical of Steve's approach for intimacy, which caused Steve to withdraw. Prior to the last year, this cycle had led to feelings of hurt and guilt, which had led to love-making. More recently, both reported being burned out and tired of trying.

Assessment of the family of origin revealed that Kevin was the older of two children. His mother was a counselor for an industrial firm, and his father was a successful, aggressive, and driven entrepreneur. His mother was critical and pedantic. Although the basic needs of the children had been met, there was little warmth or nurturance within the family. The parents were bonded to each other to the exclusion of the children. Both parents had high expectations for the children.

Steve was the second oldest of four children. His father was moderately successful as a restaurant owner, and his mother was a housewife. Because of long work hours, Steve's father was seldom at home, and Steve's role in the family was that of "counselor" to his mother, listening to her complaints about her absent husband.

Kevin stated that he had "announced" his gayness to his parents, and the topic had never been discussed since. Steve suspected that his parents knew; however, he had never discussed the topic with his parents or siblings.

Freud (1975) was the first to suggest that clients view therapists as parent-like figures. Others have referred to this process as transference. Guntrip (1969) suggested that clients are actively seeking a parental relationship that will somehow correct past deficiencies and failures of their parents' rearing skills. The delineation of the process of reparenting is one of the major contributions of Kirschner and Kirschner (1986).

Indeed, it appeared that parental deficiencies had led to Kevin's inability to allow intimacy, although he wanted it, and to Steve's weakness and ineffectuality in his life, as well as his inability to penetrate Kevin's defensiveness. Therefore, the therapist wanted to develop a reparental stance with both, a procedure that required joining each person by approximating the relationship between the client and that parent with whom he was bonded.

Initially, conjoint therapy sessions focused on bonding with both Steve and Kevin. Bonding with Steve required a warm, caring stance, because this approximated his relationship with his mother, along with a penetrating, toughening approach to help him develop a stronger ego. Bonding with Kevin required more emotional distance, because this approximated his relationship with his mother, along with periodic praise of his achievements and of him as a person. The therapist did considerable work on getting them to spend more time together and have more fun. Sexual activity between them resumed, and because Steve was fearful of losing Kevin, he terminated his extrarelationship affair. Kevin was encouraged to join Alcoholics Anonymous to control his drinking.

Although Kevin rarely talked to his parents, Steve talked to his mother every other day. In fact, Kevin was jealous of the closeness between Steve and his mother. The therapist began making Steve aware of how draining his relationship with his mother was, how she told him all of her woes in order to get sympathy and nurturance. It was suggested that he was actually married to his mother, instead of his lover. As Steve appeared to be unable to separate from his mother, the therapist adopted a paradoxical approach and suggested that he visit his mother for an entire weekend. When he returned, he was depressed and drained. It was then suggested that his calls to his mother be limited to once weekly.

The therapist had hypothesized that Steve had recreated his parents' marriage, casting Kevin as his critical father and himself as his withdrawing, self-pitying mother. When Steve withdrew from Kevin, Kevin perceived Steve as his uncaring, indifferent mother. On the foundation level, Steve experienced a basic fear of abandonment, which kept him dependent on Kevin.

In working with a gay person, the single most important intervention that can be made is to facilitate their "coming out" (Coleman, 1982; Dank, 1971), or disclosing their gayness to family and friends. Failure to come out is to live in a shroud of dishonesty, guilt, shame, and self-hatred, which impedes self-acceptance and the ability to develop intimacy with a lover.

In therapy, Kevin was encouraged to buy two books for parents of gays and begin more open discussions with his parents about his gayness. He did both and even persuaded them to join Parents of Gays, a support and educational organization. Similarly, Steve came out first to his mother, which facilitated his differentiation, and later to his father. His mother felt hurt, and his father threatened never to speak to him again. This blew over with time. Whereas Kevin and Steve had previously visited their respective parents separately, they began alternating visits to their parents and visited as a couple. Tension began to subside, and each began to be accepted by the other's parents. Because neither of them had any support from other gay people, the therapist encouraged them to become members of a gay couples recreational group, where they could meet, have fun with, and learn from other gay couples, as well as develop new interests. Additionally, both were involved in the AIDS Task Force, an organization devoted to education about the AIDS issues and to the provision of direct services to persons with AIDS. They both began to make new friends and develop a "gay family."

Because Kevin was emotionally closed, just as his mother was, the therapist wanted to help him regress to his childhood, or relate to the child within him, to provide reparative emotional input and to increase his openness to intimacy. The therapist used a benevolent, fatherly approach. With time, Kevin became more emotionally open and accepted the nurturing from the therapist that he had never received from his mother. As he began to drop his defensiveness against intimacy and to the very nurturing he needed, he became more spontaneous and playful, which had positive effects on his relationship with Steve.

In addition, the therapist worked with Steve on his distantiated relationship with his divorced wife and 8-year-old son. Several conjoint sessions with Steve and his wife resolved considerable anger and hurt feelings. Visitation arrangements were made such that Steve could regularly be with his son and resume his role as a father. As Kevin was Steve's current primary lover, the therapist assisted Kevin in assuming the role of step-parent. Effort was invested in bonding Kevin to the son, as well as in facilitating the relationship between Steve and his son.

As indicated earlier, Steve had identified with his weak mother. Thus, he came across as a weak man. In order to strengthen his ego, the therapist adopted the posture of a friendly disciplinarian. Because Steve was very unhappy with his occupation, he decided during the course of therapy to make a major career change. He had always dreamed of opening a bed and breakfast place. He did so, with the financial help of Kevin.

After 1 year of individual treatment, conjoint sessions were again held. Although there had been some focus on the couple in their respective individual treatments, more direct work was done in conjoint therapy to help them understand each other's dynamics, deficiencies, and needs—based on the family of origin. Kevin learned that Steve needed considerable benevolent discipline to get him moving toward the satisfactions that he wanted, and Steve learned that Kevin needed to be nurtured. They became effective in reparenting each other and filling each other's needs, thus programming themselves for an intramarital coalition. As they assumed more responsibility for each other, the frequency of the therapy sessions was reduced. After 2½ years of treatment, it was agreed to terminate therapy.

CONCLUSION

Gayness strikes at the very heart of a man's identity. It determines in large part who his friends are, what his support system is, who his relationship partner is, and how he views himself in the world at large. Dealing with this identity and its conflicts enables a gay man and a gay couple to blossom and potentiate their growth as individuals and as a couple. Ignoring or judging such issues produces little positive growth and, in all probability, harms the emotional health of a gay man and his partner.

As gay men are continuing to accept themselves on deeper levels, they are developing primary relationships with each other more and more often. A clinician who works with gay couples must be aware of the gay experience in our society and work actively with these couples to reduce the effects of homophobia. Family therapists have much to offer gay couples, because the overlap between gay and straight couples is considerable. Therapists must realize that relationships are important, if not necessary, and that the quality of the relationship is the issue, not the gender of the people in that relationship. Prejudice and bigotry have no place in therapy, as the ultimate purpose of therapy is the promotion of intimate relationships that work.

REFERENCES

American Psychiatric Association. (1980). *Diagnostic and statistical manual of mental disorders: III* (3rd edition). Washington, DC: Author.

Bell, A.P., & Weinberg, M.S. (1978). *Homosexualities: A study of diversity among men and women.* New York: Simon & Schuster.

Bowen, M. (1978). *Family therapy in clinical practice.* New York: Jason Aronson.

Brown, L., & Zimmer, D. (1986). An introduction to therapy issues of lesbians and gay male couples. In N. Jacobson & A. Gurman (Eds.), *Clinical handbook of marital therapy* (p. 1). New York: Guilford Press.

Coleman, E. (1982). Developmental stages of the coming out process. In J.C. Gonsiorek (Ed.), *Homosexuality and psychotherapy: A practitioner's handbook of affirmative models* (p. 19). New York: Haworth Press.

Dank, B.M. (1971). Coming out in the gay world. *Psychiatry, 34,* 180–197.

Forstein, M. (1986). Psychodynamic psychotherapy with gay male couples. In T.S. Stein & C.J. Cohen (Eds.), *Contemporary perspectives on psychotherapy with lesbians and gay men* (p. 1). New York: Plenum.

Freud, S. (1975). An outline of psychoanalysis. In J. Strachey (Ed. & Trans.), *The standard edition of the complete psychological works of Sigmund Freud* (Vol. 23, pp. 141–208). London: Hogarth Press.

Guntrip, H. (1969). *Schizoid phenomena, object relations and the self.* New York: International University Press.

Harry, J. (1982). Decision making and age differences among gay male couples. *Journal of Homosexuality, 8,* 9–21.

Kaslow, F. (1981). A diaclectic approach to family therapy and practice: Selectivity and synthesis. *Journal of Marital and Family Therapy, 7*(3), 346–351.

Keller, D. (1986). Abstract of a workshop on comprehensive family therapy for gay male clients. *Association of Lesbian and Gay Psychologists Newsletter, 12*(2), 7.

Kirschner, D., & Kirschner, S. (1986). *Comprehensive family therapy: An integration of systemic and psychodynamic treatment models.* New York: Brunner/Mazel.

Mahler, M. (1980). On the first three subphases of the separation-individuation process. *International Journal of Psycho-Analysis, 53,* 333–338.

Maracek, J., Finn, S.E., & Cardell, M. (1982). Gender roles in the relationships of lesbians and gay men. *Journal of Homosexuality, 8,* 45–49.

Maslow, A. (1962). *Toward a psychology of being.* Princeton, NJ: D. Van Nastrand Co.

Maylon, A.K. (1982). Psychotherapeutic implications of internalized homophobia in gay men. In J.D. Gonsiorek (Ed.), *Homosexuality and psychotherapy: A practitioner's handbook of affirmative models* (p. 7). New York: Haworth Press.

McWhirter, D., & Mattison, A. (1982). Psychotherapy for gay male couples. In J. Gonsiorek (Ed.), *Homosexuality and psychotherapy: A practitioner's handbook of affirmative models* (p. 3). New York: Haworth Press.

McWhirter, D., & Mattison, A. (1984). *The male couple.* Englewood Cliffs, NJ: Prentice-Hall.

Morin, S., Charles, R., & Maylon, A. (1984). The psychological impact of AIDS on gay men. *American Psychologist, 11,* 1288–1293.

Moses, A.E., & Hawkins, R.O., Jr. (1978). *Counseling women and gay men.* St. Louis, MO: C.V. Mosby.

Nichols, S., & Strow, D. (1984). *Psychiatric implications of the acquired immune deficiency syndrome.* Washington, DC: APA Press.

Peplau, L.A. (1982). Research on homosexual couples. *Journal of Homosexuality, 8,* 3–8.

Peplau, L.A., & Cochran, S.D. (1981). Value orientations in the intimate relationships of gay men. *Journal of Homosexuality, 6,* 1–19.

Plummer, K. (1975). *Sexual stigma: An interactionist account.* London: Routledge & Kegan Paul.

Reece, R. (1979). Coping with couplehood. In M. Levine (Ed.), *Gay men* (p. 11). New York: Harper & Row.

Silverstein, C. (1981). *Man to man: Gay couples in America.* New York: William Morrow.

Stein, A. (1980). Comprehensive family therapy. In R. Herink (Ed.), *The psychotherapy handbook* (p. 16). New York: New American Library.

Stein, T.S., & Cohen, C.J. (1984). Psychotherapy with gay men and lesbians: An examination of homophobia, coming out, and identity. In E.S. Hetrick & T.S. Stein (Eds.), *Psychotherapy with homosexuals* (p. 7). Washington, DC: APA Press.

Thoreau, H.D. (1966). *Walden and civil disobedience.* New York: Norton.

8. Couples Therapy with Cocaine Abusers

Stephanie S. O'Malley, PhD
Assistant Professor
Department of Psychiatry
Substance Abuse Treatment Unit
Yale University School of Medicine
New Haven, Connecticut

Thomas R. Kosten, MD
Assistant Professor
Department of Psychiatry
Substance Abuse Treatment Center
Yale University School of Medicine
New Haven, Connecticut

With its allure of glamour and prestige, cocaine has attracted increasing numbers of Americans—often with very unfortunate consequences. It has been estimated that nearly 40 million Americans have tried cocaine, and 20% of these have become regular users. Of the regular users, 25% progress to compulsive use. Given that there are currently nearly 2 million compulsive cocaine abusers, the need for effective treatments is clear (Gawin, 1986).

To date, the only studies of psychological interventions with cocaine abusers have examined the efficacy of the behavioral method of contingency contracting (Anker & Crowley, 1982) and a treatment approach involving frequent supportive psychotherapy, self-control strategies, exercise therapy, and hospitalization during detoxification (Siegel, 1982). Despite the burgeoning literature on marital and family treatments for alcoholism and other forms of drug abuse (e.g., Kaufman & Kaufmann, 1979; Stanton & Todd, 1982), we know of no previous report focusing on marital therapy with cocaine abusers.

COCAINE ABUSERS

As cocaine has become more readily available at lower prices, there has been an increase in the heterogeneity of cocaine abusers. The majority of users who

Note: Support for this work has been provided to TRK through a Research Career Development Award from ADAMHA #K02-DA0012.

121

sought treatment in the early 1980s tended to be affluent and successful. They had generally used cocaine intranasally at first, but in severe cases, had progressed to freebase smoking. Polydrug use was uncommon, although some concurrent marijuana and alcohol abuse may have occurred during cocaine binges. The use of cocaine was associated with narcissistic issues related to achievement and self-image. Abusers, particularly male abusers, tended to be controlling in their marriages; they "wanted it all" and often had it all in terms of money, power, and fast-paced lives.

In recent years, cocaine abuse has become more common among less affluent and more maladjusted users for whom separation from the family of origin is a major issue, even when they are married. This group of abusers tends to be younger and is more likely to freebase cocaine or use it intravenously, sometimes with heroin. Indeed, polysubstance abuse is not uncommon. These users are much like opioid abusers in their patterns of drug abuse and in their marital dynamics. Although the media spotlights the cocaine abuse of stars like Len Bias, Don Rogers, and Richard Pryor, this less affluent group may now comprise the majority of compulsive users (Kandel, Murphy, & Karus, 1985).

ADAPTIVE FUNCTIONS OF COCAINE ABUSE

Mr. Y. was a 30-year-old Italian-American married for 5 years. He sought treatment for cocaine abuse after he had used freebase cocaine for 2 years. His wife, a 28-year-old German-American housewife, was 6 months into her second pregnancy. They had a 3-year-old son who was reported to be doing well at home. Both Mr. Y.'s mother and Mrs. Y.'s parents lived in the same town as the patient and visited Mrs. Y. and their grandson several times per week.

Mr. Y. worked as a manager in the family business and was very well paid. His father, the founder of the company, had died 2½ years before this treatment episode, and an important issue for the family was control of the business. Mr. Y's mother and older brother, who had not been active in the business before, had become increasingly involved after the father's death. These two family members were concerned that Mr. Y. was not managing the company well. He would spend hours in his locked office, refusing to answer telephone calls or knocks on his door. Unanswered mail accumulated, and important meetings were missed. Unknown to them, Mr. Y. was in his office smoking freebase cocaine.

While using cocaine, Mr. Y. was uninterested in the rest of the world, including the business and his family. He would go home late at night and "crash" on the living room couch without seeing his son or talking to his wife. This behavior had continued for most of the 2 years that he had been using cocaine, although it had become more extreme during the few months before he sought treatment.

Mr. Y. had been introduced to freebase cocaine by a high-school friend at a party shortly after his father's death. He found that he liked the high and felt that it improved his performance at work, at least initially. At the beginning, he used cocaine episodically in weekly binges of 12 to 24 hours, but he was using it daily toward the end of his cocaine career. After 2 years, he was more than 1 million dollars in debt for cocaine purchases and sought treatment because of intense pressure from cocaine dealers who wanted to be paid. He had to tell his family about his large debts in order to protect himself from death threats; in the process of telling them of his need for money, he was also forced to reveal his problem with cocaine. While his mother and brother had suspected his involvement with cocaine, his wife denied any previous awareness of the problem.

Treatment began with a 6-week hospitalization in a general psychiatric setting because of the intense dysphoria that followed cessation of use. Mr. Y. was initially suicidal, but this was resolved within 2 days. His mood gradually improved, along with his appetite and his ability to sleep. Tricyclic antidepressant medication (desipramine) was prescribed after the first week in order to help with his continued depression and cocaine craving. After the first week of inpatient treatment, couples meetings began. Following discharge, weekly meetings were held for 6 months in an outpatient setting.

Mr. Y.'s mother and brother were included in the first couples meeting. While the mother focused on the terrible mess of the business, the wife's concern was with her own children and their home. The wife repeatedly stated that she did not care about the financial arrangements and business problems of the family. She felt that Mr. Y.'s mother and brother oppressed him rather than relieving the intense pressure under which he worked. In general, the wife was focused on her pregnancy and felt that Mr. Y.'s unavailability at home was a major problem that had been caused by his difficult work schedule. The mother and brother felt that the wife was naive and unwilling to face her husband's drug problem.

Clearly, there were significant problems both on the job and at home. Mr. Y. was not available in either setting because of his cocaine use. It was quite evident that the family of origin and the family of procreation each blamed the other for Mr. Y.'s cocaine abuse. Therapy focused on the couple, in particular, on encouraging the wife to assert some control in the relationship and to stop externalizing responsibility to her in-laws. Instead of blaming her husband's family for his drug use, Mrs. Y. needed to take a more active stance against the cocaine abuse and acknowledge her own capacity to influence her husband.

Mr. Y. was a successful, achievement-oriented man, who had been very effective with the company as the director of sales. His ability to make quick decisions was a significant asset, but he had limited patience with difficult employees and business negotiations. This style of conducting business was also reflected in his marriage. His wife was rather passive; although energetic in their social life, she had no desire to know their financial status or to share in major decisions about purchases or household needs. She had never seen any bank statements, income tax forms, charge account bills, or other indications of their vast accumulated debt. This was consistent with the dynamics of her family of origin in which her father, a prominent attorney, was domineering and managed the family's affairs with no help from her or her mother.

Because of Mrs. Y.'s inability to accept much responsibility and her belief that his family was responsible for her husband's problems, the financial affairs of Mr. and Mrs. Y. were placed in the hands of an attorney whom both Mr. Y. and his mother trusted, rather than directly under the control of Mrs. Y. This action was essential to prevent financial disaster and to minimize the potential for cocaine abuse relapse by limiting available funds.

Couples treatment then addressed issues related to the pregnancy, contingency plans should Mr. Y. abuse cocaine again, and an improved alliance between the wife and her mother-in-law. In all these areas, the couple needed to become more balanced in their responsibilities. Mrs. Y. needed to adopt a tougher stance in setting limits for her husband. Most of these issues were addressed through routine structural family therapy techniques, including the assignment of tasks to be performed at home and reviewed in the therapy sessions.

Cocaine abuse was monitored through laboratory studies of urine specimens obtained three times per week; study results were made available to the couple's therapist. It had been agreed that, if cocaine were detected in the urine, Mr. Y. was to be hospitalized for at least 4 weeks. This contingency plan was necessary and was utilized 1 month *after* the baby was born. Cocaine use had been suspected in the 2 weeks prior to the delivery when Mr. Y. failed to give two urine specimens, but the therapist compromised by having Mr. Y. return to the agreed schedule of urine monitoring. In retrospect, this was the first test of the limit-setting ability of the therapy. A compromise was necessary at that time because Mrs. Y. did not want Mr. Y. in a psychiatric hospital when she delivered. Limit setting can be effective only if the drug-free spouse supports it.

As in work with alcoholic couples (e.g., Steinglass, 1979), one of the essential aspects of treatment with cocaine abusers involves a thorough assessment of the adaptive functions that the cocaine use serves for the individual and for the couple. A number of potentially adaptive consequences, such as avoidance of responsibility or negative emotions, modulation of intimacy, and identification with a peer group, can maintain the substance abuse.

Certain pharmacological aspects of cocaine may create relatively unique consequences. Until the advent of greater publicity about the pitfalls of its use, cocaine had been glamorized in our culture. Indeed, many of the acute effects of cocaine usage in its early phase, such as elation, heightened confidence, friendliness, self-admiration, and appetite suppression, are admired traits in our society (Gawin, 1986). In contrast to the sedative effects of alcohol, the stimulant effects of cocaine may initially enhance a user's performance in activities such as work, creative thinking, and the management of several responsibilities. Ironically, as the cocaine abuse progresses, functioning deteriorates substantially in all of these areas.

These attributes of cocaine can be seductive for achievement-oriented individuals and couples. Upwardly mobile individuals with narcissistic concerns, like Mr. Y., become involved with cocaine socially at first, but escalate their use when cocaine seems to help them overcome performance anxieties and feelings of inadequacy. The spouses of these individuals often have narcissistic concerns of their own that leave them little tolerance or empathy for either negative affect or the expression of insecurity by the abusers. At least initially, cocaine keeps the abuser feeling more confident and effective, thereby reducing the demands on the nonabusing spouse for emotional intimacy and reciprocity in the relationship. In this way, cocaine abuse modulates intimacy in the marriage.

Mr. Y. became involved with cocaine shortly after the death of his father. His wife, a relatively self-centered woman, was emotionally unavailable to him. His cocaine use initially helped him to avoid the pain caused by his father's death and to overcome privately experienced insecurity about his ability to manage the company. His wife preferred to see him as a successful person who could manage with little assistance from her. This may have contributed to her denial of his drug problem until she was confronted with information about death threats and his million dollar debt.

PARALLELS TO OTHER ADDICTIONS

Mr. D. was in his early 20s and had been married for 2 years. The youngest of three children, he had a close relationship with his mother, but his father was distant and authoritarian. Mr. D. and his wife sought treatment after he had used drugs for 8 years; during the prior 18 months, he had been using cocaine intravenously.

Mrs. D. was a bookkeeper who also managed the couple's finances. She was surprised every month when she tried to balance their checkbook and found hundreds of dollars missing. When she questioned her husband about this, he told her that she must have made a mistake. Her denial of financial problems was so extreme that she did "not notice" for over 2 months that her husband had lost his job and was no longer contributing a paycheck. She also avoided any questioning about his involvement with drugs, even though she knew that he had used drugs before they were married and was herself the daughter of an alcoholic father. Overall, she saw herself as a caring person who had responsibility for the couple's welfare and blamed herself for incidents that were obvious signs of her husband's relapse into drug abuse. This role appeared to be an extension of a parental or parentified role that she had played with her own mother in dealing with an alcoholic father.

When a friend of Mr. D. finally brought Mr. D.'s drug abuse into the open, explaining that Mr. D. arrived home so late because he was trying to get more drugs, Mrs. D. reacted with extremely maternal behavior—she set out to find him and "bring him home." She actually ventured into the dangerous parts of the city where drugs could be obtained in order to find her husband. She found him, threatened to divorce him, and demanded immediate change. He responded by crying and asking for forgiveness. She then took him home; washed, dressed, and fed him; and took him to the treatment program the next morning. Her strikingly parental behavior suggested that they had a primitive mother-child relationship.

Treatment for Mr. D. and his wife first required education about signs of drug abuse and a confrontation of her denial of the problem. While Mr. D. remained contrite and superficially cooperative for the first 3 weeks of outpatient treatment, he became increasingly rebellious and threatened to stop the couples treatment. This was the first test of his wife's limit setting; although her insistence on his participation in treatment recast him in the child role, this was necessary in order to continue the therapy. Only later could the therapist address the development of a more symmetrical, adult relationship. An important therapeutic activity during the early sessions was the identification of responsibilities that Mrs. D. could give up most easily and that Mr. D. could assume.

The therapists also used genograms to examine cross-generational patterns of behavior and substance abuse. This technique made it possible to focus not only on Mr. D.'s permanent child role with his mother in his family of origin, but also on Mrs. D.'s parents and her role as a parental child in her own family of origin. The couple's relationship was in many ways an extension of the parent-child family patterns that were easily observed within both families of origin.

The dynamics of the marriage of Mr. and Mrs. D. bear similarities to the interactional patterns that have been described in families of opiate addicts and couples with an alcoholic member. Bepko and Krestan (1985) suggested that it is common for alcoholics to be under-responsible for themselves, while their nonalcoholic spouse is overly responsible for others with regard to task and emotion. Because they have no choice but to take charge, nonalcoholic spouses can assume power without challenging their selfless and giving self-image. Likewise, alcoholics can assert their independence by drinking, while the drinking simultaneously disables them and allows them to be dependent on the spouse.

In a similar way, cocaine can shift the balance of power in a marital relationship. As the abuser becomes increasingly compromised by his or her drug abuse, the nonabusing spouse may assume greater responsibility and authority in the relationship. In the case of Mr. D., his wife was overly responsible in the relationship and perceived herself as a very caring person. Her husband's addiction justified her controlling and infantilizing behavior. From Mr. D.'s perspective, the drug use was at times a means to rebel and at other times a means to elicit care.

In presenting a model of opiate addiction, Stanton and associates (1978) posited a homeostatic addiction cycle between addicts and their parents in which there is a nurturing mother and a detached, policing father. Parallels of these parental roles are often found in the marital relationships of male addicts (Kosten, Jalali, & Kleber, 1982). Specifically, the nurturing and forgiving wife may become policing when a financial or legal crisis forces her to confront the addiction. Consistent with this model, the dysfunctional interactions between Mr. and Mrs. D. were rooted in interactional patterns in their families of origin. To the extent that this couple is representative, it is perhaps not surprising that a large proportion of cocaine abusers and their spouses are adult children of alcoholics, with estimates of their numbers ranging up to 50% (Gawin & Kleber, 1986). Consequently, an assessment of multigenerational patterns of substance abuse and of the individuals' roles within their family of origin can provide clues to help therapists understand the marital relationship.

DENIAL OF COCAINE USE

The spouse's denial of the abuser's cocaine use is often most significant during the first phases of the addiction. It is often the revelation of significant financial problems incurred as a result of cocaine use or evidence of sexual indiscretions committed while under the influence of cocaine, rather than issues regarding the actual quality of the relationship, that motivates the spouse to insist on treatment. The length of time from the initial recreational use to severe adverse consequences and the ultimate seeking of treatment usually ranges from 2 to 5 years (except in the case of crack usage when the progression is much quicker). By the time couples seek treatment, the consequences of the cocaine use are generally so severe that it is difficult to deny the problem, at least for the moment. Continued denial by the spouse may be a greater problem in the families of alcoholics and polysubstance abusers. In the case of alcoholism, for example, the progression of the disorder to the development of severe consequences often occurs over a longer time period of 5 to 20 years, thereby providing greater opportunity for gradual homeostatic adjustment by the family.

Many cocaine abusers approach treatment with ambivalence, even though they recognize that they have lost control of their drug use (Rounsaville, Gawin, & Kleber, 1985). This ambivalence regarding treatment and their denial of the seriousness of the drug problem often remain important issues during the course of treatment. The abusers hold on to the hope that they can reduce their cocaine use to manageable levels and thereby make it unnecessary to give up the positive feelings that they attribute to cocaine. Cultural perceptions of cocaine as a nonaddicting drug and the belief that glamorous people use it as a recreational drug also contribute to their denial.

In light of these factors, the therapist's task is to "puncture the patient's idealized, romantic view of cocaine or of himself as a cocaine user" (Rounsaville et al., 1985, p. 176). This may be accomplished by obtaining a careful history of the consequences and realities associated with past cocaine use and frequently contrasting these with the perceived benefits of continued cocaine use. Referrals to Cocaine Anonymous groups may be helpful in this area. Attendance at Cocaine Anonymous meetings can sometimes elicit conditioned craving, however, and the therapist should be sensitive to this possibility.

ACHIEVEMENT AND MAINTENANCE OF ABSTINENCE

Once the cocaine abuser agrees to treatment, efforts must be made to achieve abstinence and prevent relapse. Abstinence can be achieved through either inpatient or outpatient treatment. Because withdrawal from cocaine is not medically dangerous, outpatient treatment can be quite satisfactory. Inpatient treatment may be necessary, however, when

- the abuser is contemplating suicide
- there are other serious psychiatric or medical problems
- there is a concurrent dependence on other drugs that requires detoxification
- outpatient treatment has failed repeatedly (Gawin & Kleber, 1987; Washton, Gold, & Pottash, in press)

Because cocaine is so highly reinforcing, it is important to restrict access to the drug. It may be necessary for the nonabusing spouse to take over the family finances in order to limit the abuser's access to large sums of money. As the abuser progresses in treatment, responsibility for these areas can be reinstituted. Antidepressant medication can be helpful in reducing the craving and anhedonia during the early weeks of abstinence (Gawin, 1986). Urinalyses and contingencies for handling relapse can be incorporated into the treatment. These strategies are not specific to couples therapy, but are also used in individual and group treatment (Gawin & Kleber, 1987).

ROUTE OF ADMINISTRATION AND MARITAL PATHOLOGY

Cocaine is typically used in one of three ways: (1) intranasally, (2) intravenously, or (3) by freebase smoking. Despite the popular belief that intranasal use produces a relatively mild form of abuse (Grinspoon & Bakalar, 1976), all three routes can result in addiction (Gawin & Kleber, 1985; Helfrich, Crowley, & Atkinson, 1983). Patterns of cocaine use differ as a function of the administration route, however, and this may have implications for marital functioning.

Mr. D. had been using a combination of heroin and cocaine called a "speedball." Injected intravenously, the combination provides the euphoria associated with both drugs without the acute dysphoria or "crash" that follows the use of cocaine alone. Like most speedball users, Mr. D. had runs of several hours during which he injected himself every 30 to 40 minutes. Daily use becomes quite common among speedballers, particularly as they become addicted to the heroin. Users addicted to heroin get sick from opioid withdrawal symptoms if they go without heroin for 12 to 18 hours.

In contrast, Mr. Y. had freebase smoking binges during which he administered cocaine every 15 to 20 minutes for as long as 3 days and then had a severe crash that sometimes led to thoughts of suicide. Pure freebase cocaine users characteristically have 12- to 72-hour binges of heavy cocaine use, followed by abstinent intervals of 7 to 10 days; they describe no craving for cocaine during these abstinent intervals. These pure cocaine users are not motivated to seek more drugs by the discomfort of opioid withdrawal.

These two patterns of use differentially affect the user's overall level of functioning. For intranasal or freebase users, periods of relatively good functioning are mixed with briefer periods of quite impaired functioning during a binge and for approximately 24 to 48 hours afterward. Intravenous cocaine users, however, gradually become totally impaired and have no periods of good functioning, because they are always seeking the opioid to relieve the pain of the withdrawal symptoms.

The differential level of impairment in abusers is often mirrored in their marital relationship. The marital interactions of those who administer several drugs intravenously exhibit more dependence and resemble parent-child interactions more closely than do those of intranasal users or freebase smokers. This is illustrated by the two couples. In both cases, however, structural family therapy techniques were used successfully to develop more symmetry in the marital relationship.

CONCLUSION

As Rounsaville and associates (1985) noted for cocaine treatment in general, the aims of couples cocaine treatment are threefold: (1) to help the couple recognize the negative effects of cocaine use and to accept the need for abstinence, (2) to help the abuser achieve and maintain abstinence, and (3) to help the couple understand the functions that cocaine use has played and to work out more adaptive means of fulfilling these functions. Structural family therapy techniques can be effective in meeting these goals.

REFERENCES

Anker, A.L., & Crowley, T.J. (1982). Use of contingency in specialty clinics for cocaine abuse. *National Institute for Drug Abuse Research Monograph Series, 41*, 452–459.

Bepko, C., & Krestan, J.A. (1985). *The responsibility trap: A blueprint for treating the alcoholic family.* New York: The Free Press.

Gawin, F.H. (1986). New uses of antidepressants in cocaine abuse. *Psychosomatics, 27*(Suppl. 11), 24–29.

Gawin, F.H., & Kleber, H.D. (1985). Cocaine abuse: Patterns and diagnostic distinctions. *National Institute for Drug Abuse Research Monograph Series, 61*, 182–192.

Gawin, F.H., & Kleber, H.D. (1986). Abstinence symptomatology and psychiatric diagnoses in cocaine abusers. *Archives of General Psychiatry, 43*, 107–113.

Gawin, F.H., & Kleber, H.D. (1987). Issues in cocaine-abuse treatment research. In S. Fischer, A. Raskin, & E.H. Uhlenhuth (Eds.), *Cocaine: Clinical, biobehavioral aspects* (pp. 174–192). New York: Oxford University Press.

Grinspoon, L., & Bakalar, J. (1976). *Cocaine.* New York: Basic Books.

Helfrich, A.A., Crowley, T.J., & Atkinson, C.A. (1983). A clinical profile of 136 cocaine abusers. *National Institute for Drug Abuse Research Monograph Series, 43*, 343–350.

Kandel, D.B., Murphy, D., & Karus, D. (1985). Cocaine use in young adulthood: Patterns of use and psychosocial correlates. *National Institute for Drug Abuse Research Monograph Series, 61*, 76–100.

Kaufman, E., & Kaufmann, P.N. (Eds.). (1979). *Family therapy of drug and alcohol abuse.* New York: Gardner Press.

Kosten, T.R., Jalali, B.J., & Kleber, H.D. (1982). Complementary marital roles in male opiate addicts. *American Journal of Drug and Alcohol Abuse, 9*, 155–169.

Rounsaville, B.J., Gawin, F., & Kleber, H. (1985). Interpersonal psychotherapy adapted for ambulatory cocaine abusers. *American Journal of Drug and Alcohol Abuse, 11*, 171–191.

Siegel, R.K. (1982). Cocaine smoking. *Journal of Psychoactive Drugs, 14*, 271–359.

Stanton, M.D., & Todd, T.C. (Eds.). (1982). *The family therapy of drug abuse and addiction.* New York: Guilford Press.

Stanton, M.D., Todd, T.C., & Heard, D.B., et al. (1978). Heroin addiction as a family phenomenon: A new conceptual model. *American Journal of Drug and Alcohol Abuse, 5*, 125–150.

Steinglass, P. (1979). Family therapy of alcoholics: A review. In E. Kaufman & P.N. Kaufmann (Eds.), *Family therapy of drug and alcohol abuse* (pp. 147–186). New York: Gardner Press.

Washton, A.M., Gold, M.S., & Pottash, A.L.C. (in press). Cocaine abuse: Techniques of assessment, diagnosis and treatment. *Psychiatric Medicine.*

9. May-December Marriages: Dynamics, Structure, and Functioning

Laura J. Singer-Magdoff, EdD
President
Interpersonal Development Institute, Inc.
New York, New York

M ay-December marriages have long intrigued the popular fancy, as evidenced by public interest in the marriages of Charles Chaplin to Oona O'Neill and of Pablo Picasso to his tragic Jacqueline, as well as by ancient tales (e.g., the story of Jocasta and Oedipus) that have enriched the fantasies of analyst and analysand. Age differences in marriage have only recently become a category of special interest to marital therapists, however.

SURVEY OF THE LITERATURE

In analyzing marital age differences among various age groups, Bytheway (1981) studied all marriages in England and Wales in 1976. According to his data, *for both sexes*, the tendency to marry a younger person peaks at 30 to 34 years of age and falls to its lowest point at 50 to 54 years of age. After the age of 34, unmarried individuals are more likely to marry someone their own age or older. This trend reverses for unmarried people of both sexes in their 50s, who are again more likely to marry someone younger. Bytheway hypothesized that, after the age of 30, single people turn to the "secondary age" group, ages 40 to 60, for potential marital partners.

Cowan (1984) conducted two studies on the perception of age-discrepant relationships. One involved adult males and females (mean age of 28 years); the other, male and female high-school students. Subjects were randomly assigned to read a brief biographical sketch and rate a couple that fell into one of five categories: (1) male and female same age, (2) male 7 years older than the female, (3) female 7 years older than the male, (4) male 18 years older than the female, and (5) female 18 years older than the male. Both adults and adolescents viewed highly discrepant relationships (i.e., those in which there was an 18-year age difference) more negatively than they viewed moderately discrepant relationships (i.e., those in which there was a 7-year age difference). Moreover, female older relationships were thought to be more suspect than male older relationships.

Males, both adults and adolescents, viewed female older relationships with large discrepancies more negatively than they viewed those with moderate differences. Females did not discriminate between these two groups. Overall, relationships in which the female was older were thought to have less chance of success than did those in which the male was older. This acceptance of the "double standard" by both adolescents and adults sanctions relationships between older males and younger females, but not the reverse.

In their study of the effects of the double standard on people's perceptions of age-discrepant couples, Hartnett, Rosen, and Shumate (1981) asked male and female college students to read vignettes describing age-discrepant couples. Half of the students received vignettes in which the male was older by 17 years, and half received vignettes in which the situation was reversed. The groups were then split again, with half of each informed that the older person was wealthy and half informed that the older person had an average income. No significant differences were found between the perceptions of older men and older women in these age-discrepant relationships. The wealthy older person was viewed more favorably than was the older person of average income, however, regardless of sex. The younger woman was viewed more favorably than the younger man by female subjects, but the male students were more supportive of the younger man. Thus, it appears that people are more favorably disposed to individuals who are similar to themselves.

Peterson (1983) investigated 79 older woman–younger man couples who were at least 10 years apart in age, labeling them the "new dyad." The women were over 40 and had lived with or been married to a partner 10 years younger than they were for a minimum of 1 year. In her study of the personality characteristics of these couples, Peterson found that these individuals were more alike than different, that they both tended to be expressive and androgynous, that they were more relationship-oriented than work-oriented, and that they subverted traditional expectations concerning gender roles and responsibilities.

According to Presser (1975), Veevers (1984), and Carter and Glick (1970), remarriages are more likely to involve an age discrepancy than are first marriages. Presser noted that this trend is consistent for both sexes; women who were married previously are more likely to marry younger men who are marrying for the first time, and vice versa.

Presser (1975) also claimed that many young women marry older men who are more intelligent and more accomplished than they are in order to raise their standard of living and enhance their social status. She pointed out the irony of these relationships, as these women actually restrict their status by giving up any educational or career goals of their own. She argued that there will be status differences between the sexes as long as there are (large) age differences in marriages and as long as women are thought to be solely responsible for child-rearing. She suggested that age discrepancies may be less significant for older women.

In a study of data gathered in the 1970 National Fertility Study, which included all ever-married women in the United States under the age of 45, Bumpass and Sweet (1972) hypothesized that there may well be some connection between age-discrepant relationships and marital instability. Their findings indicated that marital instability increases when there are significant discrepancies in the ages of husbands and wives. They claimed that age differences decrease "value consensus," particularly in an era of rapid social change. In addition, they hypothesized that people who enter age-discrepant marriages may have personal qualities that increase the risk of marital difficulties. Finally, they suggested that age discrepancies may upset the power structure in a family, especially when the wife is older. This study appears to reflect a cultural bias against older women.

In quite a different vein, Foster, Klinger-Vertabedian, and Wispe (1984) examined the effects of age differences on male longevity and concluded that 50- to 79-year-old men who were married to younger women tended to live longer than did those who were married to older women. Although the authors advised caution in interpreting this finding, they speculated that it may be the result of premarital selection factors and the effects of the couple's postmarital interaction. They did, however, conclude that age difference is related to longevity and that this relationship merits further study.

PROJECTIVE IDENTIFICATION AND SPLITTING IN THE TREATMENT OF AGE DISCREPANT COUPLES

Couples' therapy from an object relations theoretical stance is psychoanalytic in its base. It includes interpretation of unconscious material. It also deals with transferential and countertransferential material. One of its major goals is the development of understanding and insight as to how earlier experiences in each spouse's family of origin, mostly repressed, are played out defensively in the marriage.

Object relations theory places an emphasis upon the earliest mother child relationship within an interaction mode. Unlike the Freudian instinctual-structural theory, it emphasizes the infant's ability to relate to and influence an external object from the moment of birth as an active participant. The infant is viewed as capable of affecting the way in which the external object, be it the mother or other caregiver, will henceforth relate to the infant. It is the earliest interactive model and often becomes the model for the interaction between spouses.

Melanie Klein (1948), an object relations theorist of the English school, described that early period of human development in which the infant does not differentiate between the self and external objects, calling it the "paranoid-schizoid" phase of infant development. During this period, the infant's sensorimotor experiences are split into those that make the infant feel good and those that make the infant feel bad. The "bad" parts of the self are "split off" and eliminated by being projected into another person. (It is important to note that Klein's object relations came out of very primitive perceptions of the infant in relationship to the mother's breasts and were viewed as fantasies by her.)

It was Melanie Klein who first described projective identification, projecting parts of one's self into an external object in an attempt to get rid of bad parts of the self by putting them into an external object and then attacking it. At the same time, good parts of the self are put outside to protect them from the badness remaining in the self. This division between good and bad self and object is called "splitting." Projective identification and splitting have been helpful constructs in the treatment of those couples in the case studies that follow.

Mahler, Pine and Bergman (1975) further clarified the concept of splitting when they identified the stages of infantile development. The stages include the autistic, the symbiotic, separation-individuation, rapprochement and the stage that they termed "on the road to object constancy." The developmental stage of separation-individuation is the period in which they observed the predominance of splitting operations, which indicate an inability to integrate self and object representations. They set the splitting into the "good" and "bad" mother and the "good" and "bad" self within the rapprochement subphase.

Developing the foregoing thesis more fully, Kernberg (1980) stressed the "continuity of the originally fused, 'bad' self-object representation of the symbiotic phase" (p. 107). Couples often employ defensive operations of splitting and projective identification as well as the defenses of denial, omnipotence, and devaluation in their interactions to each other and to the marital therapist.

Slipp (1984) placed the phenomenon of projective identification within dyadic or triadic relations and within fluid ego boundaries so that "good or bad aspects of the self or the object can be put into another" (p. 57). He added that "pressure is exerted to induce the other to think, feel, or behave in a manner that is congruent with the internalized self or the object" (p. 57). Furthermore, according to Slipp, there must be a close, continuing relationship between the projector and the object in order to permit reinternalization through identification of the evoked behavior of the object. It thus becomes the task of the marital therapist to help the person who is the object of the other's projection to psychologically process that projection. If the processing is successful, the object can moderate the feelings that have been raised by being the object of projections. The marital therapist may be called upon to model modified ways of processing the projections and demonstrate alternative ways of interacting with the projector. The modeled interactions shown by the therapist can help the projector to reexperience his or her projections in a way that is new and not as damaging to either partner.

MAY-DECEMBER RELATIONSHIPS

The following case studies depict couples who have not sufficiently differentiated between self and object representations (Stolorow & Lachman, 1980), have difficulty tolerating ambivalence, and are troubled with a split between good and bad objects and good and bad self representations (Kernberg, 1980).

> Johnny and Joyce walked into the therapist's office, sat down, and smiled at each other. Still holding Joyce's hand, Johnny turned to the therapist.
>
> Johnny: I've been thinking all week about your fee. It's too damned high. Not even medical doctors I know charge as much as you do . . . and don't you give professional discounts? Where do you get off charging those fees, and you're only a psychologist and a marriage counselor. . . . (*He continued to barrage and attempted to bait the therapist.*)
>
> Joyce: For heaven's sake, Johnny, you make me sick, you're such a cheapskate. You always go on about how much things cost, and how much money everyone else has, and how they earn more than you do, and how stupid they are. You make me feel so ashamed. (*Louder and louder and more frenzied were her cries.*)

Johnny (*dropping Joyce's hand and shouting*): You have some nerve talking to me that way. All you know how to do is spend money, going shopping all the time. I never should have introduced you to designer clothes. Now you're not married to me, you're married to Bloomingdale's and Bergdorf's. What do you think I'm made of? Where do you get off talking to me that way? You brought nothing into this marriage. Where would you be if my family didn't have money?

Therapist: Johnny, it sounds as though you don't feel that you are worth the money it takes to have the therapist you have chosen. Or, maybe for once you would like me to know how it feels to feel powerless and in somebody else's control.

If the therapist had offered to send him to someone else at a lower fee, the therapist would be reinforcing his idea that he was not worth much. If the therapist had offered to lower the fee, the therapist would not be worth much.

Johnny was a 43-year-old dentist who had just opened his practice. His office was in a building owned by his father, and he was dependent on his father's generosity. He saw his father as angry, rebellious, very powerful, and controlling, and he felt powerless, weak, and devalued around him. His mother was a beautiful woman, but she was angry, withdrawn, unavailable, and intellectually quite limited. "She was a model," said Johnny, "and used her beautiful face to ensnare my father for his money."

Joyce, 26, worked with Johnny as his receptionist. She was of a different faith than Johnny, but he had converted to Joyce's faith to spite his father and to feel more powerful for once. He married Joyce because he felt sorry for her. From a poor home, she had an alcoholic father and a depressed mother. Each had been married previously. They had been married to each other for 2 years, and they said that their relationship had been intense and happy for 6 months. Both were possessive and very jealous of any relationship that either had with anyone else.

Johnny had played the role of Joyce's tutor and tried to control her in much the same way that his father tried to control him—by withholding money and belittling her—and in much the same way that he had tried to devalue and belittle the therapist. The powerless, impotent rage that he turned on the therapist was intense. The therapist became the recipient of the devalued, denigrating aspect of the self, split off, and projected on the therapist as Johnny and Joyce projected it on each other and the marriage. This was a difficult couple; it helped that each was in individual treatment.

Donald, 50, was an attractive, brilliant entrepreneur and millionaire. Precise and deliberate, he looked for challenges, was sharp and volatile, and had difficulties in his relationships with his children and friends. His second wife, Debbie, was 40; her marriage to Donald was her first.

Debbie was slight and outdoorsy. She loved sports; Donald hated them. She was in advertising, was interested in photography, tended to be introspective, and had a number of close female relationships. She was the first child of a schizophrenic mother. Her mother had been hospitalized when Debbie was 7 years old and again when she was 10. Debbie was always deeply ashamed of her mother. She hated her father, perceiving him as mean, angry, hateful, and hurtful to her, to her brother, and especially to her mother. Debbie believed that her family was different from other families, not as good as her friends' families. She felt a good deal of guilt about her feelings and was certain that she had "something mean and vicious inside, and that getting too close to anyone would let them know there was nothing inside, just a phony, empty." Debbie used splitting, denial, and projective identification defensively to keep her "bad self" contained.

Donald's first marriage had ended in a very bitter divorce that left him feeling that all women were after his money and were not to be trusted. Moreover, he felt very self-righteous about his attitude. His first wife was like his father, who had humiliated him, belittled him, and abandoned him. This internal object, this split-off part acted toward Debbie as his father had acted toward him when he was a little boy.

Debbie felt that Donald had a whole underside (similar to her own) that she could not trust; she said that he could be mean, like her father. "He's a nice man, but he's also a pushy, obnoxious man. He's provocative. He baits and pushes his opinions on people, wants things done his own way; his way is the only right way. He'll push and feel that right is on his side." Debbie also felt that right was on her side. "He acts like I haven't said anything; it makes me in touch with some crazy area in myself. He makes me angry, makes me want to take revenge."

Donald carried around his internal image of the angry, strong father who had belittled and criticized him. Because nothing he had ever done had been "good enough" for his father, Donald felt attacked, demeaned, and inadequate whenever Debbie disagreed with him or wanted something different from what he had provided. He stormed, raged, pushed, and provoked until she responded; then, he would back off. As his father did to him, so he did to Debbie. As Debbie's father did to her, so she did to Don. Both also carry the loving parts of their early object representations, however, and sometimes have been able to be warm, affectionate, and loving to each other.

Condemning and competitive, Debbie had grandiose fantasies and felt superior to all her women friends. She remembered being petrified as a child that she had eliminated her mother when her mother was institutionalized and she took over as the woman of the family. She had tried to dominate and control in the guise of sweetness and compliance. When she became angry, she went into a panic and felt bad, horrible, wicked, and unlovable. She had been working very hard in individual therapy to resolve and integrate primary ambivalent feelings.

Debbie had been unable to make a lasting commitment to marriage until, through therapy, she learned that she had always been searching for the idealized image and, in this way, had protected herself from her own split-off, enraged, antiloving feelings. Only when she was consciously aware and could accept the "mean self" could she take the risk and marry Donald. Marriage to him seemed less risky than did marriage to someone her own age, because Donald had more experience than she, had two grown children, and had achieved considerable success in the marketplace.

The women in these cases, and in the 25 May-December relationships analyzed in this study, all appeared to have had critical, demanding mothers and remote or unpredictable fathers. The older men that they married had fathers who were highly competitive and presented a strong macho image; their mothers were narcissistic and dependent.

The women were frightened about individuating and achieving some degree of independence. Unconsciously, they were highly competitive with their mothers; were drawn to men with rescue fantasies; and appeared to have transferred their symbiotic attachment from their mothers to older, protective, potentially nurturant, but unusually critical men. Even those mothers who had been independent in their actions and those who had worked to take care of their children when the father was weak, not present, incapable, or perhaps dead were frequently critical of their daughters and implied that it was not particularly desirable to be independent, that it was better to "have a man who will take care of you and look after you."

The husbands in the May-December marriages that were studied were at least 10 years older than their wives. The individuals in the study group ranged in age from 26 to 76 years of age, and there were age differences in the couples of 10 to 30 years. Eight of the couples had been married from 2 to 22 years; one woman had been widowed after a 20-year marriage to a man who was 28 years her senior. One was divorced after a marriage that had lasted for 15 years and included two children; another, after a marriage that had lasted 1½ years and included one child. Two other couples had been living in age-discrepant relationships for more than 4 years.

Some of the "December" men might be categorized as very special, very wealthy, or very celebrated. The majority were competent and able, but not extraordinary. The "May" women, bright and appealing, included a city politician and a debutante.

Men in our culture have traditionally married women who are their age or younger. This holds for both first marriages and for remarriages. When divorced men remarry, they often select women who are considerably younger than their first wives. The last 40 years have witnessed an increase in the life span for both sexes, and women are living longer than are men (Riley, 1983). As a consequence of both tradition and demographics, the field of eligible spouses has been decreased for women, but is increasing for men.

DECEMBER-MAY RELATIONSHIPS

There has been an increase in the number of women who marry or have long-term, committed relationships with men who are younger than they are. Older women–younger men relationships can be described as December-May relationships. The women in this category tend to be either helping professionals (e.g., therapists or teachers) or creative and performing artists. Their concerns are similar to those of women in age-homologous marriages: stability, acceptability, and self-esteem (Derenski & Landsburg, 1981). Ranging from real estate entrepreneurs to cabinetmakers, the younger men that they choose appear sensitive and nurturant, and they especially enjoy being valued and appreciated. As Bernard (1972) observed, "there is no 'natural' age difference between spouses one way or the other [and] it would make sense to have an older wife and a younger husband, since, in our day, women tend to outlive men" (p. 167).

Paul, 34, and Patricia, 40, were both slender, attractive, creative, and articulate people who had been married for 10 years. They had one son who was 2½ years old. When Pat met Paul, she was 28 years old, and he was 22 years old. Pat had had a series of relationships, lasting from 1 to 4 years, with husbands of her friends.

Pat introduced Paul to sexual intercourse. As the sexual initiator, Pat controlled their relationship. Paul was content as the passive follower. Pat kept Paul's irrational temper tantrums in check, thus keeping his aggressive impulses under control. In fact, Pat wished to control and possess Paul exclusively. She became angry, frightened, and dismayed when he formed relationships with his colleagues at work; she reacted by exhibiting narcissistic withdrawal tendencies, denying her deep dependence. Through emotional distancing, Paul helped Pat to maintain her ego boundaries and kept her from merging with him (Kernberg, 1980).

Pat's professional competence as a free-lance writer was very important to her. It satisfied her omnipotent fantasy of being totally self-sufficient. A few years ago, her professional competence had been challenged because there were few free-lance jobs. She had become very upset and depressed, felt impotent, and been in a rage because she could not control the work situation.

Paul, a very capable illustrator, had his own fantasy of being omnipotent and self-sufficient. Involved in a deep gender identity conflict, Paul was the eldest of the three sons of a cold, enormously successful, internationally famous father who called him "skinny" and "unmanly." At the same time, his mother called him her "prince." He carried his paternal object with primitive injunctions to be great, powerful, and physically attractive. He was very involved in sports, where he was pressured to be killingly competitive, just as he was professionally. A loss was experienced as a deep blow.

Pat was the younger daughter of a cold, unemotional mother who, like Paul, was always physically present but emotionally remote. She had always seen herself as a little girl, skinny and unattractive, as her father, an automotive worker, described her. Burdened, martyrlike, self-involved, and self-absorbed, her father had been very angry with Pat when she left home at 16 years of age.

Pat hated and feared her hysterical underpinnings and anxieties. She could be calm, albeit disdainful, when Paul exhibited his fears. When Pat was in control of herself, Paul felt reassured, saw her as all good, and believed himself very lucky in his family and, especially, in his life style. This worked for him until his anxieties erupted about the level of his performance, which was never good enough in work or sex. When he became uncertain, fearful, or anxious, Pat became frightened and contemptuous. She hooked into his own self-contempt, and he became enraged with her. They had screaming matches in which each threatened to leave. When he failed at work, at sports, or in sex, he ceased to be that source of power and perfection on which she depended. Both needed him to be powerful and perfect, yet sufficiently under her control for her to avoid feeling weak, frightened, helpless, and humiliated (Kernberg, 1980).

Both Paul and Pat had been raised in an environment inimical to their legitimate growing developmental needs. They were both carrying a great deal of ambivalence and had invested each other with a great deal of hate. The ensuing guilt that they experienced inside themselves and from each other toward the self resulted in a cycle of projective identification and introjection. Although each had preserved a workable amount of ego through splitting and each was a socially and intellectually competent adult, there was an impoverishment in their most intimate object relations. They vacillated between idealization and denigration, overvaluation and devaluation. Paul had married his cold, powerful, critical father and his indulgent mother; Pat had married her cold, ungiving mother and her weak, rageful father (Slipp, 1984).

It was nonetheless comfortable for Pat to take the initiative with a passive younger man whom she felt she could control. He was most appreciative of her sexual competence and gentle guidance.

Jimmy, a 32-year-old medical supply salesman, was young and good-looking with light brown wavy hair and hazel eyes. At 28 years of age, he had married a woman 6 years younger than he was; that marriage had lasted for 6 months. As soon as he was divorced, he married Jenny, a teacher 8 years his senior. Jimmy was the youngest son of a blue-collar, alcoholic father of whom he was very much ashamed. His family was very poor. The two older sons were "very wild." Jimmy was the "good" one—good grades in school, good in sports, and a good sense of humor. He wanted to be in the public eye as a broadcaster or an actor. Friendly and charming, he was very success-oriented and had dreams of a career in the entertainment industry.

His mother was a strong woman, who looked like a delicate Magnolia blossom in danger of being crushed. Like that other southern belle Scarlett O'Hara, however, she was vain, beautiful, and tough. When she was in her 50s, she went back to school, got a job, divorced her husband, and took care of herself and her sons. At 65 years of age, she had a face lift and married for the third time. She continued to keep her weight at a delicate 90 pounds to match her tiny 5 foot 2 frame.

When Jimmy married Jenny, his family could not understand it. She was an attractive women, but 8 years older than Jimmy. A combination of sophistication and crudity, she appeared very self-confident. Her insecurities were manifested in her need to be in control. This appeared to suit Jimmy, however. She put him on display by saying such things as "Tell them what you said to me last night that was so hilarious it brought me right out of my terrible mood." His humor came out at her prompting; she helped him to perform. He became her baby; she adored him and provided him with emotional supplies that were not forthcoming from his narcissistic mother. At this stage in their marriage, they appeared to meet each other's needs: hers to be the controlling bandmaster, his to be the applauded and special performer.

The women in the December-May group apparently had unavailable, narcissistically involved mothers and highly competitive fathers who were high achievers and with whom the women tended to identify. The men in these relationships had powerful mothers and passive-aggressive fathers, some high achievers. Some of the women who had been involved in briefer relationships reported that their support network was conducive to experimentation. Not only did they feel that their friends (mostly women friends) had accepted their relationships, but also they felt that they had benefited from their relationships with younger men, whom they described as freer and not afraid to be expressive and nurturant. It appears that although there may be some degree of pathology, attempts to rectify early environmental deficits have been somewhat successful in these December-May relationships.

THEORETICAL GUIDELINES FOR TREATMENT INTERVENTIONS

In the preceding cases and in other cases in which the personality structures are similar, the following theoretical guidelines have been effective for treatment interventions:

1. offering an empathic, supportive environment without interventions in the beginning stages
2. containing the projective identifications, processing them, and responding to them in a nonhostile manner that allows for re-internalization of a benign response, interpreted and discussed at a symbolic verbal level
3. facilitating separation from a symbiotic mother (spouse) in the struggle against unacceptable dependency by facilitating acceptance of appropriate dependency needs and wishes
4. aiding the ability to tolerate and live with disappointments; giving up the need for perfection, as modeled by the therapist's ability to accept therapeutic imperfections; and enabling each spouse to give up the idea of a perfect being (e.g., the "transmuting internalization" of Kohut [1971, 1984])
5. helping each spouse to work through ambivalence, to understand early antecedents of love and hate splits, and to distinguish between external omnipotent forces and internal powerful affects
6. assisting couples in the integration of loving and hating self-representations and other representations as a precondition for establishing ego identity and an internal world of object relations in depth (Kernberg, 1980)

CONCLUSION

In age-discrepant relationships, the double standard seems to be applied consistently in that general acceptance is greater for older husband–younger wife marriages. If society were open-minded enough to regard age differences as a matter of taste and of preference, rather than as an intrinsic right or wrong, options might be increased for women and there might be more older women–younger men marriages. If and when women attain higher status at work and in relationships, how will power relationships in marriage be affected? This is an area that could certainly benefit from greater attention.

REFERENCES

Bernard J. (1972). *The future of marriage*. New Haven, CT: Yale University Press.

Bumpass, L., & Sweet, J. (1972). Differentials in marital instability. *American Sociological Review*, *37*, 754–766.

Bytheway, W. (1981). The variation with age of age differences in marriage. *Journal of Marriage and the Family*, *7*, 923–927.

Carter, H., & Glick, P. (1970). *Marriage and divorce—A social and economic study*. Cambridge, MA: Harvard University Press.

Cowan, G. (1984). The double-standard in age discrepant relationships. *Sex Roles*, *11*, 17–23.

Derenski, A., & Landsburg, S. (1981). *The age taboo: Younger men older women relationships.* Boston: Little, Brown.

Foster, D., Klinger-Vertabedian, L., & Wispe, L. (1984). Male longevity and age differences between spouses. *Journal of Gerentology, 39*(1), 117–120.

Hartnett, J., Rosen, F., & Shumate, M. (1981). Attribution of age discrepant couples. *Perceptual and Motor Skills, 52*, 355–358.

Kernberg, O. (1980). *Internal world and external reality.* New York: Jason Aronson.

Klein, M. (1948). *The psychoanalysis of children.* London: Hogarth Press.

Kohut, H. (1971). *The analysis of the self.* New York: International Universities Press.

Kohut, H. (1984). The curative effect of analysis: The self psychological reassessment of the therapeutic process. In A. Goldberg & P. Stepansky (Eds.), *How does analysis cure?* (pp. 98–100). Chicago: University of Chicago Press.

Mahler, M.S., Pine F., & Bergman, A. (1975). *The psychological birth of the human infant.* New York: Basic Books.

Peterson, S.H. (1983). The new dyad: Older women and younger men. *Dissertation Abstracts International, 45*, (10B), 3322–3323.

Presser, H.B. (1975). Age differences between spouses. *American Behavioral Scientist, 19*, 190–205.

Riley, M.W. (1983). The family in an aging society. *Journal of Family Issues, 4*(3), 439–454.

Slipp, S. (1984). *Object relations: A dynamic bridge between individual and family treatment.* New York: Jason Aronson.

Stolorow, R.D., & Lachmann, F.M. (1980). *Psychoanalysis of developmental arrests.* New York: Universities Press.

Veevers, J.L. (1984). Age discrepant marriages: Cross national comparisons of Canada/American trends. *U. Victoria, British Columbia Social Biology, 31*(½), 18–27.

Index